IMAGES
of America

LOWER
NORTHEAST
PHILADELPHIA

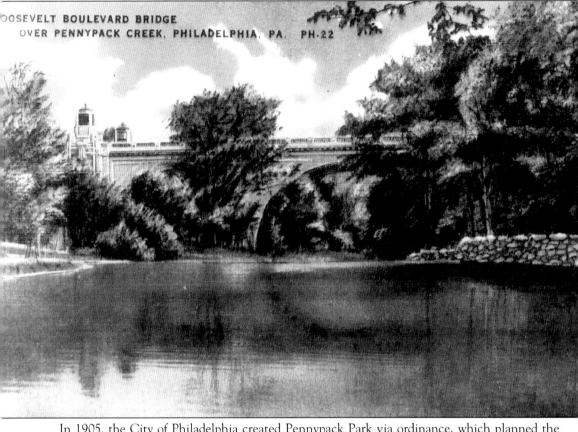

In 1905, the City of Philadelphia created Pennypack Park via ordinance, which planned the acquisition of what would become a 1,600-acre park, equivalent to 20 percent of the Fairmount Park system. This is larger than most parks across the country, including New York's Central Park. Shown here is the bridge over the Pennypack Creek at Roosevelt Boulevard.

IMAGES
of America

LOWER
NORTHEAST
PHILADELPHIA

Louis M. Iatarola and Lynn-Carmela T. Iatarola
for the Historical Society of Tacony

ARCADIA
PUBLISHING

Published by Arcadia Publishing
Charleston, South Carolina

Printed in the United States of America

Library of Congress Catalog Card Number: 2004114584

For all general information contact Arcadia Publishing at:
Telephone 843-853-2070
Fax 843-853-0044
E-mail sales@arcadiapublishing.com
For customer service and orders:
Toll-Free 1-888-313-2665

Visit us on the Internet at www.arcadiapublishing.com

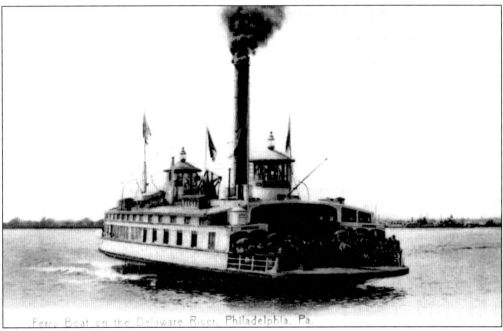

Ferry Boat on the Delaware River, Philadelphia, Pa.

Seen above is a postcard depicting a ferryboat on the Delaware River. Until the railroad connected directly into Center City Philadelphia just before the Centennial Exposition in 1876, Tacony served as the terminus of the railroad for passengers from New York. Ferries would pick up passengers at Tacony to travel into town. Consequently, the community came into its own as land between the railroad and river developed. Ferries also became an important mode of travel for Northeast Philadelphia residents prior to the construction of the Tacony-Palmyra Bridge in 1929. The location of this bridge at Levick Street followed the course of the old Tacony-Palmyra Ferry Service. (Courtesy of Tina Lamb.)

Contents

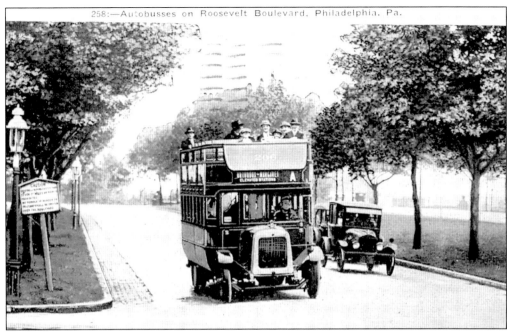

This postcard, from c. 1920, depicts Roosevelt Boulevard handling traffic consisting of an automobile and double-decker passenger bus heading to the Orthodox-Margaret Elevated Station. The sign on the left cautions vehicle operators that "driving or riding faster than seven miles per hour is prohibited." (Courtesy of David A. Rizzo.)

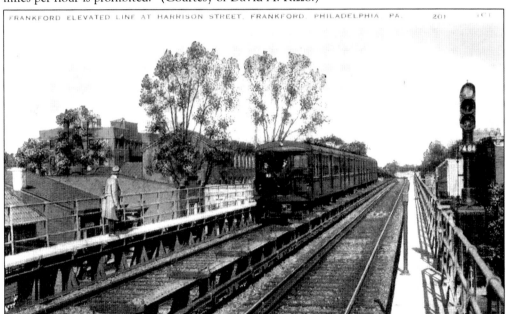

FRANKFORD ELEVATED LINE AT HARRISON STREET, FRANKFORD, PHILADELPHIA, PA.   201

The construction of the Frankford Elevated Railway began in 1905 and was completed to Bridge Street in 1922. Utilizing a new single steel support system, this railway was designed to allow more natural light onto the bed of Frankford Avenue. A five-day celebration was held to commemorate the occasion, which forever changed the landscape of Northeast Philadelphia. Seen here is an elevated train near Harrison Street in 1922. (Courtesy of Dennis Lebofsky.)

INTRODUCTION

Through images reflecting over three centuries of history, this book explores the evolution of the lower half of an area that today represents a vital and invaluable component of Philadelphia's economic well-being, in terms of both commerce and tax revenue. In its earliest days, Northeast Philadelphia was a sparsely populated wooded area with the creeks, streams, and Delaware River serving as its lifeblood. Most inhabitants were descendants of Swedish settlers or those granted land by William Penn or his associates. Along the Pennypack and Frankford Creeks, the natural flow of water powered the mills, which helped populate the areas closest to them, resulting in the original towns eventually known as Holmesburg and Frankford. Little remains of the gristmills and textile mills that fortified and perpetuated the simple lives of generations who lived in these towns for over a century. However, the villages spawned over 150 years ago by increasingly diverse employment and transportation opportunities continue to serve as stable population centers in a greater urban environment. Stretches of Frankford Avenue in both Holmesburg and Frankford contain buildings that have been in continuous use since the early 19th century.

The Pennypack Creek and wooded park that serves as its natural buffer became part of the city of Philadelphia's Fairmount Park system a century ago, and has prospered since the creation of Friends of the Pennypack over 50 years ago. Its streams, creek, plant life, and wildlife are physical reminders of the days when wilderness prevailed in Northeast Philadelphia. A visit to the park on a clear day is all one would need to see why John Audubon chose the creek's banks to study and paint birds in the 19th century. Prior to the consolidation of the city and county in 1854, the areas covered in this book were situated within Oxford Township and Lower Dublin Township with the dividing line being Cottman Avenue, formerly known as Township Line Road.

Tacony and Wissinoming came into their own in the mid-19th century, first as summer retreats with complementary recreational uses and then as centers of industrial strength. The advent of the railroad gave these areas two key components of efficient industrial operations at the time—river access and railroad frontage. By the beginning of the 20th century, industries large and small dotted the landscape along the Northeast's Delaware riverfront. The success of these many industries, most notably the Disston Saw Works in Tacony, led to the development of Wissinoming and Tacony as "towns within a town." Henry Disston laid out a cozy factory town for his workers, and Wissinoming developed into a family-based, working-class community whose religious diversity earned it the nickname "Holy City."

Torresdale served primarily as a summer resort area for wealthy businessmen based in or near Philadelphia. At the beginning of the 20th century, the easternmost portion of the area was known as "Casino Town." To this day, most of the area continues to be characterized by detached single-family homes and has remained primarily residential and institutional in nature. Torresdale is certainly the most unchanged of all the neighborhoods studied in this book.

In the early 1900s, three developments changed the social fabric of Philadelphia forever. In 1903, Roosevelt Boulevard was connected with the city at Hunting Park Avenue, near Broad Street. In 1922, the Market-Frankford Elevated was completed, which extended from Sixty-ninth Street in West Philadelphia north to Bridge Street in Frankford. In 1929, the Tacony-Palmyra Bridge opened to traffic and physically connected Philadelphia's growing population center with the state of New Jersey.

With these transportation enhancements came unparalleled municipal growth between 1930 and 1960. The community of Mayfair, situated west of Tacony and south of Holmesburg, became home to thousands of uniform row homes on manicured lawns with virgin sidewalks. The undeveloped areas of Holmesburg, Frankford, Wissinoming, and Tacony saw similar development, and as the years progressed such development sprawled north and west. Accompanying this population explosion was the need for supporting services, which resulted in the commercial development of Roosevelt Boulevard and along the former Township Line Road, now Cottman Avenue, west of Roosevelt Boulevard. Now known as the Bustleton-Cottman shopping district, this planned commercial center has grown to become the third largest shopping area in Philadelphia at 107 acres.

With the exception of Roosevelt Boulevard, Northeast Philadelphia's main artery and a chapter in itself—a common thread linking the remaining chapters together—is Frankford Avenue (state Route 13). Originally a trail established by Native Americans, this road was known in previous incarnations as the King's Highway, Bristol Pike or Turnpike, and Main Street. So important was this well-traveled pathway that William Penn gave strict orders to have a stone bridge built over the Pennypack Creek not long after arriving. In 1756, the first stagecoach serviced the King's Highway, which got its name because it linked the English government headquarters at Upland (now Chester), Pennsylvania, and New York. During Colonial times, curved stone markers were installed at one-mile increments along the roadway to delineate the distance from Center City. In 1803, King's Highway became a toll road with tollgates and houses springing up every five miles from Front Street to Morrisville, Bucks County. Lafayette made a ceremonial passing along the road en route to Holmesburg in 1824, as did Gen. Ulysses Grant on his way to Andalusia in 1866. Although the gates and markers are gone, numerous physical remnants of the 19th century and even a few from the 18th century remind us of the days when this "Main Street" served as the social and economic center for generations of hardworking townspeople.

It is the authors' sincere hope that all who read this book will come away with a more profound sense of area history and will better understand the place Northeast Philadelphia holds in the evolution of the city of Philadelphia and the United States. We would be remiss if we did not recognize Dr. Harry Silcox, whose publications about Northeast Philadelphia history were the first to stimulate public awareness of the area's rich heritage. Prior to his efforts, some of which were done in concert with local historical societies and historians, most Philadelphians thought the city's true history extended no farther north than Spring Garden Street, let alone north of Frankford Creek. Dr. Silcox has contributed countless hours and resources in promoting the efforts of the Historical Society of Tacony, and through his enlightened work has left an indelible mark in the hearts and minds of all who call Northeast Philadelphia home. We would also like to thank the many contributors of images who are credited throughout this book. Their willingness to pass on valued private collections for future generations to appreciate will be rewarded by the knowledge that countless readers will experience both joy and fascination by perusing this treasured collection.

We hope that this sampler of Lower Northeast Philadelphia communities will continue to enlighten and inspire both local and non-local residents. These communities and the people within them continue to make history every day, contributing in a major way to the stability and appeal of the city of Philadelphia as a unique destination and one-of-a-kind "city of neighborhoods."

One

FRANKFORD

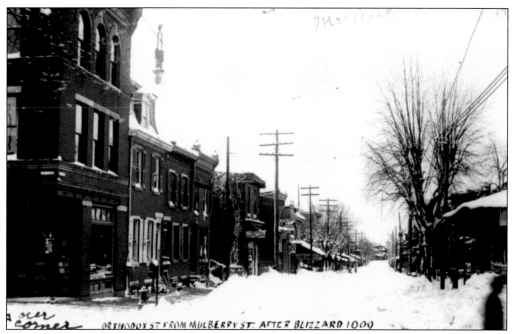

The name "Frankford" was first seen on a map prepared by Thomas Holme in 1684, as the name of the creek that ran through this village to the mouth of the Delaware River. Manor of Frank was the name given by the Society of Free Traders to the area's land purchase from William Penn. Seen above is a snow-covered Orthodox Street as seen from Mulberry Street around 1910. (Courtesy of Robert Morris Skaler.)

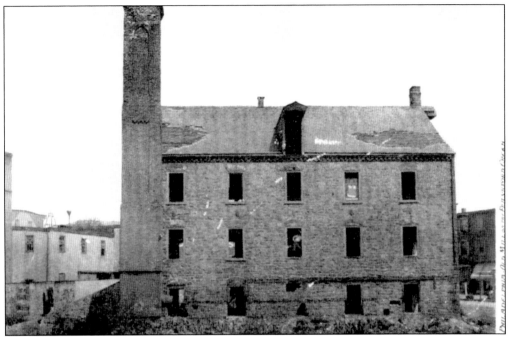

The old mill depicted in the postcard above was erected along the Frankford Creek, east of today's Frankford Avenue, by Swedish settlers around 1660. Operated by water from the creek, the mill was used to grind wheat for making flour and meal. William Penn sold the mill to the Society of Free Traders, and it was subsequently passed on to a variety of operators. (Courtesy of Robert Morris Skaler.)

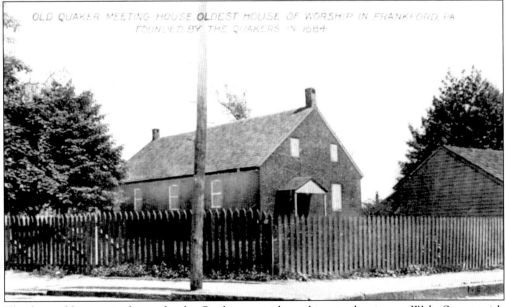

The first public meetinghouse for the Quakers was a log cabin on what is now Waln Street, with the First Oxford, and later, Frankford Friends meeting recorded there in the summer of 1683. The building seen here was built in 1775. A rear addition was constructed in 1881. (Courtesy of Bruce Conner.)

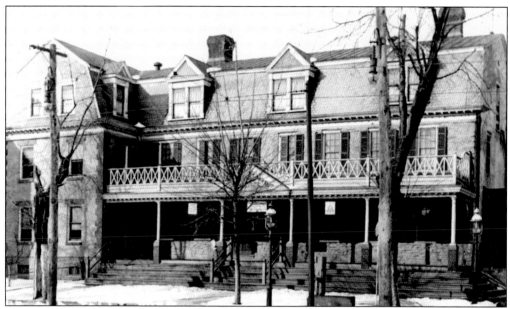

The Jolly Post Hotel was built in 1682 for use as a post office and public gathering place, and it was later expanded for use as an inn. It is believed that postmaster Henry Waldy (also spelled Waddy) resided here, at King's Highway (Frankford Avenue) and what is now Orthodox Street. George Washington stopped here several times on excursions to New York. The building was demolished in 1911. (Courtesy of Bruce Conner.)

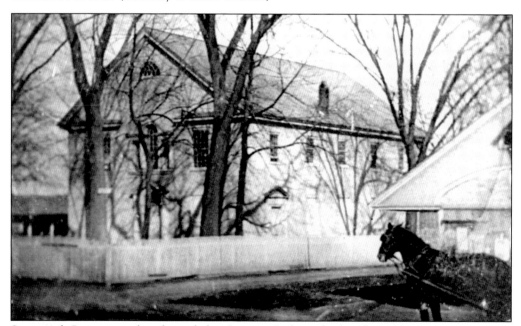

Swiss and German settlers formed the German Reformed Church and built their church at the northeast corner of Church Street and Main Street (now Frankford Avenue) in 1770. The church was built on land originally purchased for use as a burial ground. The adjacent lot served this purpose, with plots selling for $3 to $5, depending on size and location. (Courtesy of Bruce Conner.)

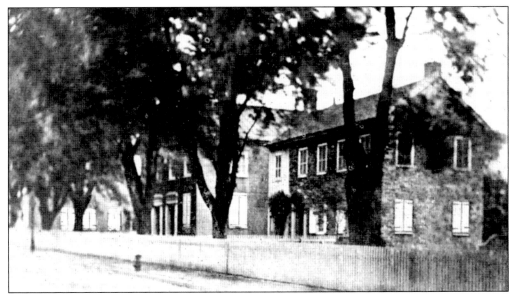

Seen above is the Frankford Academy, built in 1799, which doubled as public meeting space on the first floor. The building's assembly rooms were earmarked as the alternate home of the Supreme Court in case of a yellow fever epidemic like that which plagued Philadelphia in 1793. The borough of Frankford was organized here in 1800. In 1829, the Rehoboth Methodist Episcopal Church purchased the property and used it for 50 years.

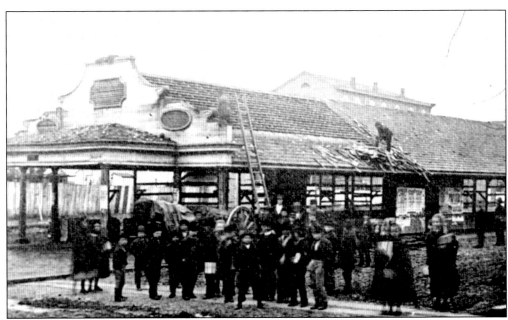

An old market house like the one seen above at Paul and Ruan Streets was rented by authorities of the borough in 1821 to ensure that its residents had an ample supply of quality meats. By law, no person could sell meats anywhere in Frankford but at the market house. Commercial activity took place every weekday from June to September and three times a week during the other months. (Courtesy of Bruce Conner.)

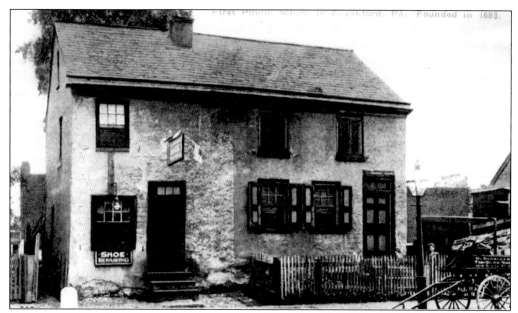

The public school system was established in the county and city of Philadelphia in 1818. Frankford formed part of the fifth section, which included the township of Oxford. The first public school in Frankford, seen above, was established in 1821 along the easterly side of Main Street (now Frankford Avenue) above Foulkrod Street. In 1822, rent for the building was $32 per year, and the student body numbered 55. (Courtesy of Robert Morris Skaler.)

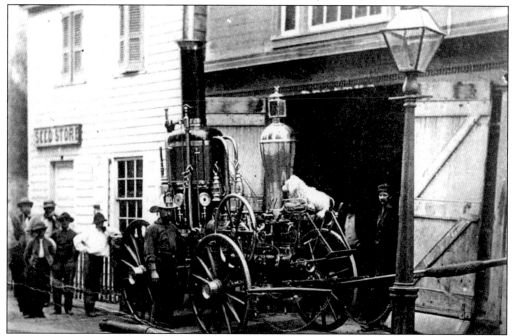

Old Decatur was known in its heyday as the Decatur Fire Company, one of a number of fire companies, such as the Washington Fire Company, which served the Frankford community. The ancient apparatus seen here could throw a 1¼-inch-wide stream of water about 100 feet. Note the customary dog atop the old engine. (Courtesy of Bruce Conner.)

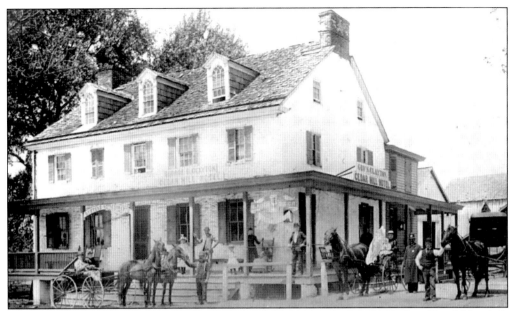

The Cedar Hill Hotel, pictured around 1900, was also known as the Robin Hood Hotel. It stood at Frankford Avenue north of Bridge Street and extended west to Bustleton Avenue. The property was sold to the Philadelphia Transit Company in 1903, and a trolley barn was constructed. Today the site is part of Bridge Street Transportation Center of the Southeastern Pennsylvania Transportation Authority (Septa). (Courtesy of Bruce Conner.)

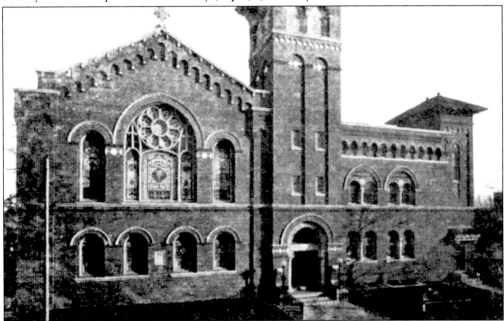

Near the intersection of Paul and Womrath Streets stood the old Frankford Academy, which was demolished by the Rehoboth Methodist Episcopal Church to expand the church building seen here. This congregation was the first to spread the word of Methodism in Frankford and helped to establish other missions, including eventual congregations at Bridesburg, Frankford Avenue Methodist Episcopal Church, and East Allegheny Avenue Church.

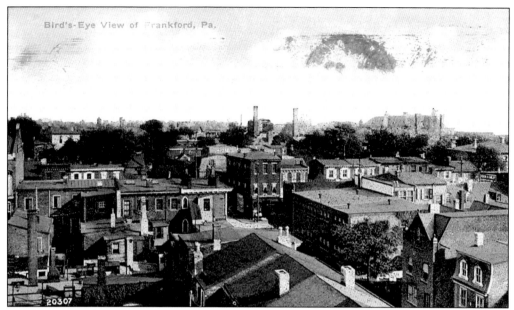

Over 150 years before the Industrial Revolution, Frankford was a thriving village with mills along the Frankford and Tacony Creeks providing stable livelihoods for working townspeople. The mills were followed by enterprises such as Isaac English's Pottery Factory, Tackawanna Print & Dye Works, and the Frankford Arsenal. The population of Frankford increased from 1,233 in 1810 to 5,346 in 1850. This view dates from *c.* 1910.

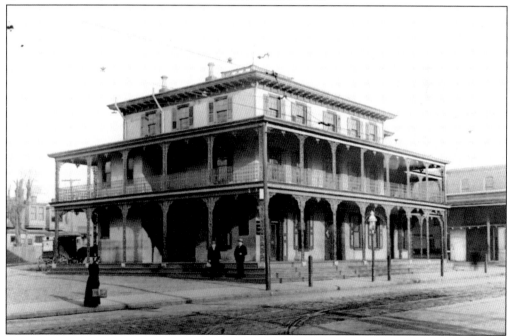

The Seven Stars Hotel was located at the southwest corner of Oxford and Frankford Avenues until it was demolished in 1926. One of the first stagecoach lines between Frankford and Philadelphia, operated by John Haines, departed from this location. The hotel was also used by farmers who would market goods in the city. (Courtesy of Bruce Conner.)

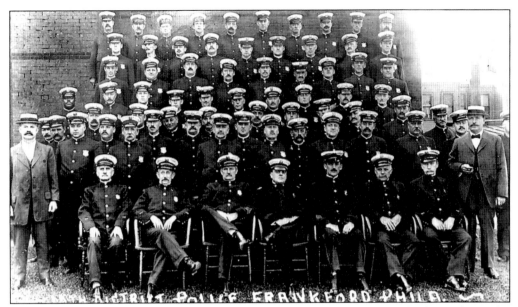

In Frankford's early days, a board of burgesses regulated improvements in the borough. By the 1820s, concern over sanitation and highway tax issues led to a movement seeking Frankford's division from Oxford Township. Upon consolidation with the city of Philadelphia in 1854, most public services became municipally managed. Seen above is the old 15th District Police Department, once housed in Frankford, around the beginning of the 20th century. (Courtesy of Dennis Lebofsky.)

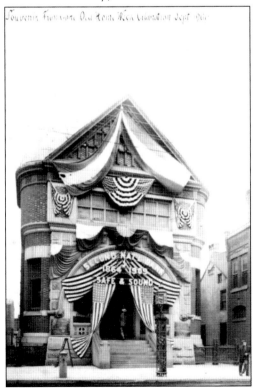

The first bank to serve the northeast section of Philadelphia was the Second National Bank, which opened in Frankford on Main Street, now known as Frankford Avenue, in 1864. The building (already 45 years old when this photograph was taken) is adorned in patriotic colors for a 1909 celebration known as Frankford Old Home Week. (Courtesy of Bruce Conner.)

The cornerstone of the tiny building for the First Presbyterian Church of Frankford was laid in 1770 along the King's Highway (later Main Street and Frankford Avenue). This church was expanded in 1810 and renovated in 1844. The edifice seen in this postcard was built in 1860. No less than 10 churches have branched from this church, including Frankford Lutheran Church and Frankford Baptist Church. (Courtesy of Tina Lamb.)

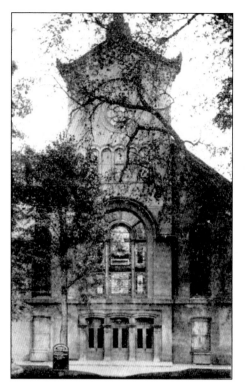

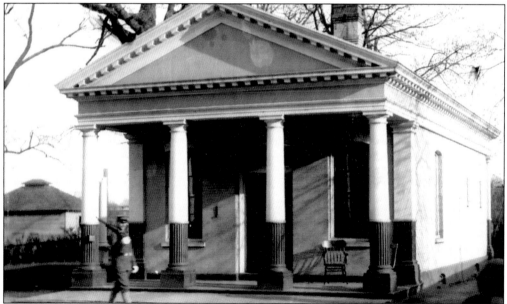

The Frankford Arsenal, pictured c. 1910 with armed guard and guardhouse, is situated where the Frankford Creek meets the Delaware River and is bounded by State (formerly Tacony) Road and Bridge Street. Pres. James Madison purchased the original 20 acres in 1816, and 42 more acres were eventually purchased by Pres. Martin Van Buren and Pres. Zachary Taylor. The Frankford Arsenal remained in use by the federal government until closing in the 1970s. (Courtesy of Dennis Lebofsky.)

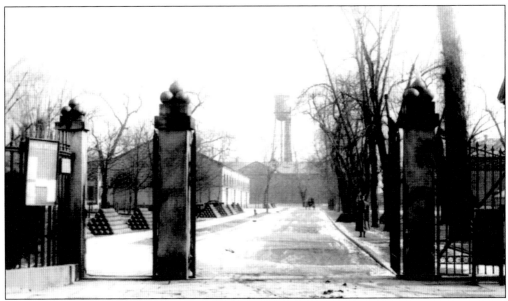

The Frankford Arsenal, seen above, proved to be a very productive facility. It was used as a depot to repair artillery and infantry equipment, to manufacture percussion powder and musket balls, and to clean and repair small arms. In 1851, the manufacture of small arms, ammunition, infantry, cavalry, and artillery equipment began. Today the property is known as the Arsenal Business Center and contains a mix of business and institutional uses. (Courtesy of Tina Lamb.)

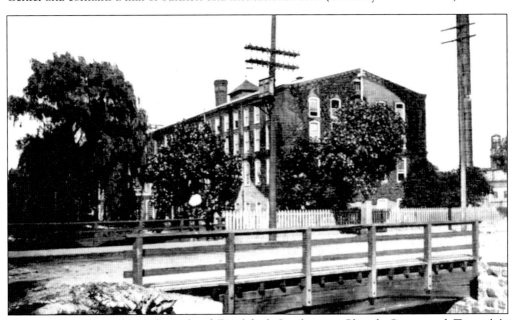

Berkshire Mills was located north of Frankford Creek near Church Street and Torresdale Avenue. As the mills and factories began to populate Frankford with residents, development first occurred primarily south of Unity Street. As manufacturing activity increased, at least nine dams served the streams in and near the Frankford and Tacony Creeks to harness waterpower. Other popular early mills included those used for tanning leather, making gunpowder, and making textiles. (Courtesy of Bruce Conner.)

St. Mark's Protestant Episcopal Church had its origins in the Tabernacle Church, which built a chapel on Franklin (now Griscom) Street between Unity and Sellers Streets. In 1845, the name was changed to St. Mark's, and a larger church was constructed in 1848. The church seen here was constructed along Frankford Avenue, north of Unity Street, in 1896 with the first services held on the first Lenten Sunday in 1897. (Courtesy of Robert Morris Skaler.)

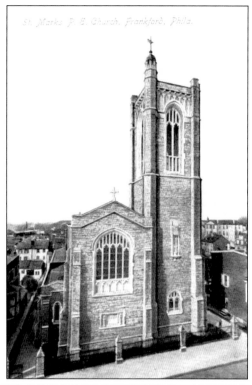

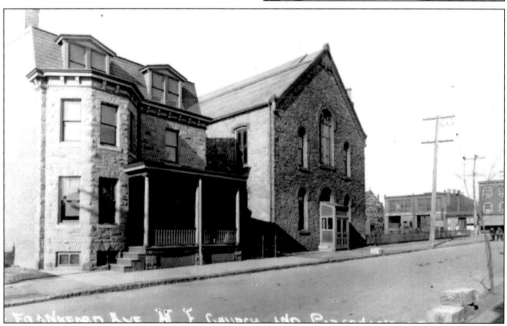

Frankford Avenue Methodist Episcopal Church was established in 1871, after a branch school of Rehoboth Methodist Episcopal School was organized. Their first church, seen above along with the parsonage, was soon erected at the southeast corner of Frankford Avenue and Foulkrod Street. The church was constructed with blue stone (gneiss) from a Frankford quarry. A new church was built in the Gothic style in 1910. (Courtesy of Bruce Conner.)

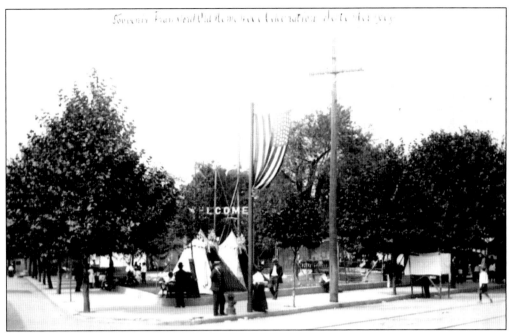

Womrath Park is a triangular swath of parkland bounded by Kensington, Frankford, and Adams Avenues. This view depicts events in the park during the 1909 Old Home Week. Favorite recreational activities at the turn of the century included picnics, traveling circuses in summer, and sledding or ice-skating in winter. (Courtesy of Dennis Lebofsky.)

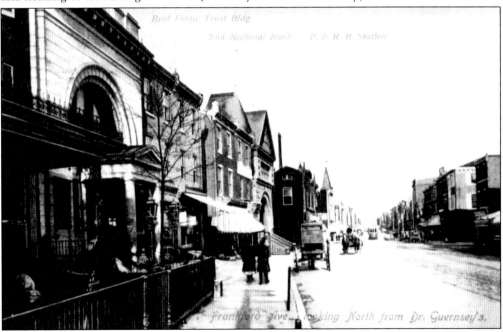

This *c.* 1910 view of Frankford Avenue looks north from near Unity Street. The scene recalls the days when the avenue seemed so much wider without the steel support structure for Septa's elevated train that extends from the south up Frankford Avenue to Bridge Street. (Courtesy of Bruce Conner.)

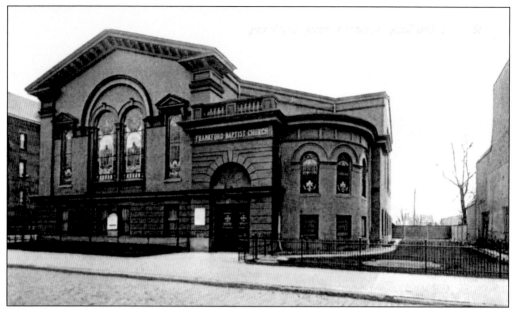

The Frankford Baptist Church was established about 1807 in a modest building at Penn and Church Streets. Various Baptist missions branched off from this church, including congregations at Holmesburg and North Frankford. A more centrally located site at Paul and Unity Streets was chosen to build a new church in 1855. On the same site in 1897, the old church was dismantled and replaced by the one seen above. (Courtesy of Robert Morris Skaler.)

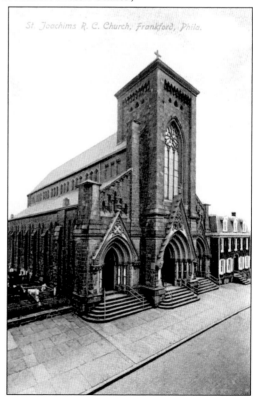

St. Joachim's Roman Catholic Church was founded in 1847 to fill the growing need for Catholic centers of worship in Frankford at the time. A small edifice on Church Street was demolished to make way for the Gothic-style brownstone building seen here. Its parochial school, at Church and Penn Streets, was considered one of the finest of its time when built in 1882.

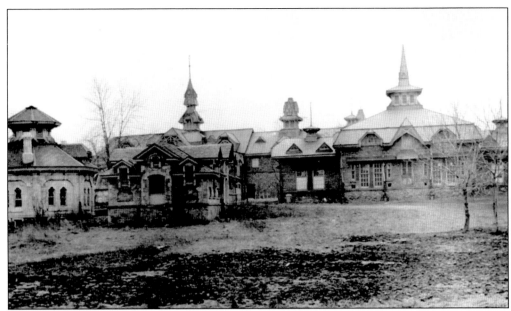

From 1900 until about 1908, the property depicted in the postcard above was situated along Oxford Avenue at the present site of Frankford High School. It was used by the Frankford Country Club, which converted the old turkey house seen on the right to a locker room. The Frankford Country Club eventually merged with Torresdale to form the Torresdale-Frankford Country Club. (Courtesy of Tina Lamb.)

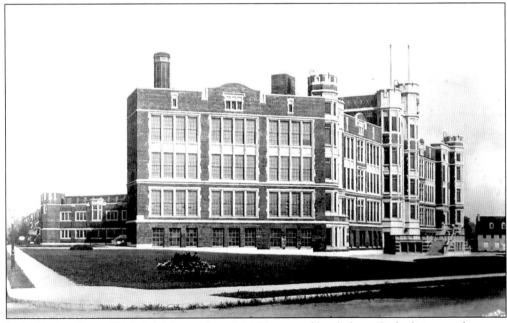

In 1909, the City of Philadelphia purchased 4.635 acres of land along Oxford Avenue between Harrison and Oakland Streets to build Frankford High School, seen here. The building was completed in 1910, and a solemn ceremony to lay the cornerstone was witnessed by the entire student body, parents, and city dignitaries. (Courtesy of Dennis Lebofsky.)

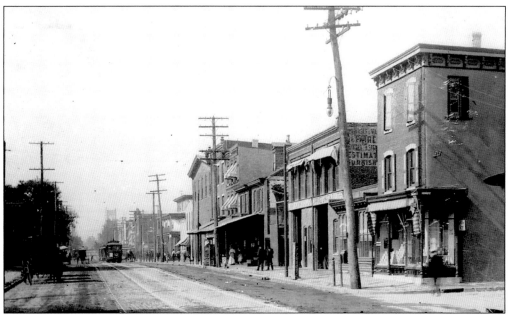

Seen above is a 1900-era postcard view of Main Street (now Frankford Avenue) looking in a southerly direction from Foulkrod Street when the only modes of travel were trolley car or horse and buggy. Foulkrod Street was named for one of the first families to settle in the area. The Roosevelt Theatre opened near this intersection and had its glory years in the 1930s and 1940s.

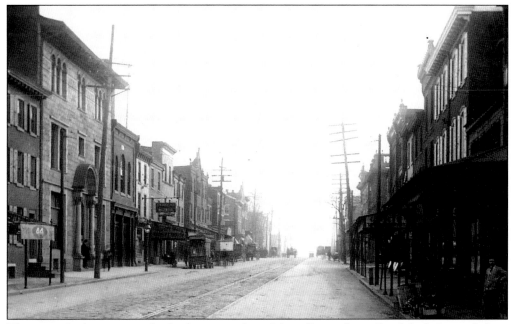

This view looks in a northerly direction along Main Street (now Frankford Avenue) from near Sellers Street. The Sellers were another old-time Frankford family. Other theaters that were located along the avenue included the Casino, near Womrath Street, the Frankford near Margaret Street, the Circle (later the Empire Theater), and the Princess Theater, located just east of the avenue on Orthodox Street.

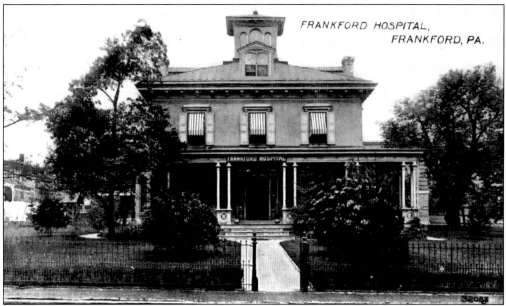

Frankford Hospital started in relatively small quarters within the old building depicted in the postcard seen above, from about 1910. Situated at the southwest corner of Wakeling Street and Frankford Avenue, this hospital has undergone significant expansions over the years and is a major presence on Frankford's landscape today. An additional campus of Frankford Hospital was established in Torresdale. (Courtesy of Bruce Conner.)

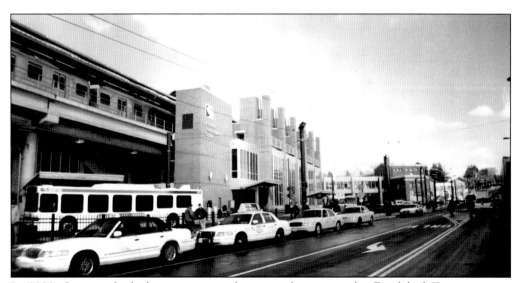

In 2000, Septa embarked on a mammoth project known as the Frankford Transportation Center, a $187 million facility designed to modernize the 80-year-old station. Located at Bridge Street and Frankford Avenue, the center serves as a hub for 16 bus routes and an elevated railway stop, catering to about 25,000 people daily. Seen here is the new center with a remnant of the old terminal at the rear.

Two

HOLMESBURG

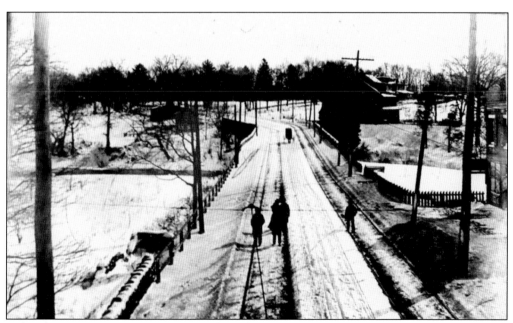

Holmesburg got its name from its founder, Thomas Holme, who was William Penn's surveyor-general. Holme was granted about 1,650 acres of land from Township Line Road (now Cottman Avenue) to Red Lion Road, west from the Delaware River. His descendants were major landowners as the area grew into a village. Seen above is Main Street (now Frankford Avenue) looking north toward the Ashburner Street curve from near Solly Avenue. (Courtesy of Rudy DeFinis.)

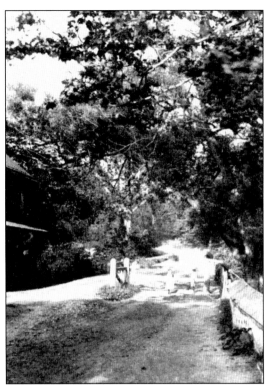

In 1683, one of William Penn's first acts was to ask the English court of Upland to build a bridge over the Pennypack where the King's Highway crossed it. This was a major obstacle to land travel along what is known today as Frankford Avenue. The first three-arch stone bridge in America, a National Engineering Landmark, was completed in 1697. This view looks south from across the bridge and tollgate toward Solly Avenue.

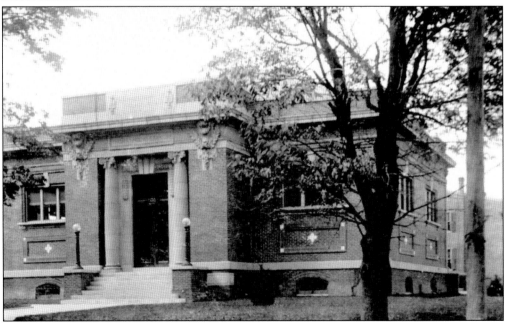

Thomas Holme eventually settled in a country-like estate on farmland along the banks of the Pennypack Creek. He called his home Wellspring and raised two sons and two daughters. Holme's original land holdings extended from the Delaware River west to where Roosevelt Boulevard is today. Pictured above is the Thomas Holme Branch of the Free Library of Philadelphia on Frankford Avenue. (Courtesy of Tina Lamb.)

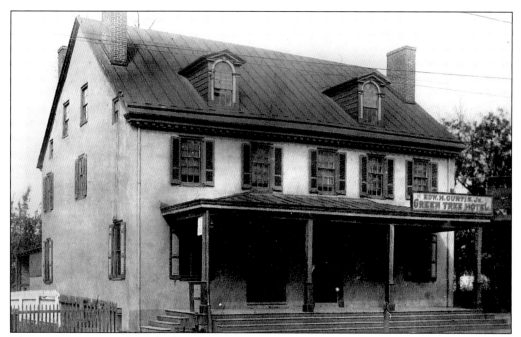

The Green Tree Hotel was built at what is now the southwest corner of Frankford Avenue and Rhawn Street in 1799. This was a popular stagecoach stop and remained in use until the early 1900s, after the trolley displaced stagecoaches as the popular means of travel. The building is in use today as an automobile tag and insurance agency. (Courtesy of Rudy DeFinis.)

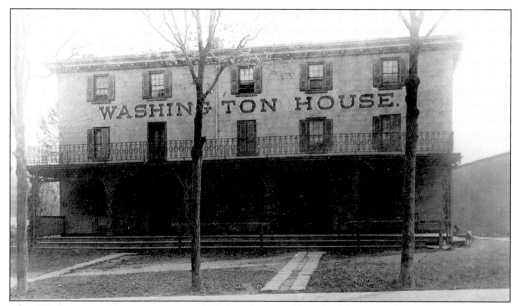

The Washington House was one of Holmesburg's oldest buildings, and for decades it was a reminder of the days when the area was known as Washingtonville. Built in 1796, the property served as a stagecoach relay station for changing horses on trips from Philadelphia to New York. The building was situated along the easterly side of Frankford Avenue, south of Welsh Road, and it was demolished in 1928. (Courtesy of Rudy DeFinis.)

27

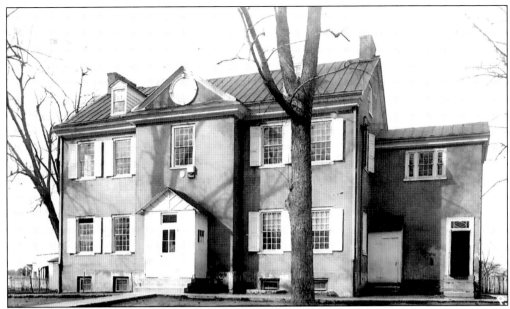

The Lower Dublin Academy began in a modest schoolhouse in 1723 and constructed this facility in 1808, utilizing stone from the nearby Holmesburg Quarry. Upon the consolidation of Holmesburg with the city of Philadelphia in 1854, the school was renamed in honor of Thomas Holme. In 1952, a modern facility was constructed west of the original school (seen here), which still stands near Academy and Willits Roads. (Courtesy of Dennis Lebofsky.)

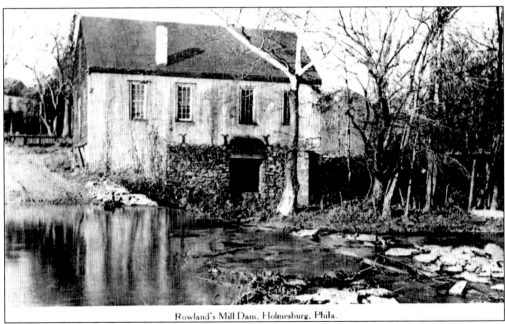

Rowland's Mill Dam, Holmesburg, Phila.

The Rowland Shovel Works was located near where Father Judge High School stands today. Its founder, Jonathan Rowland, was a descendant of John Rowland, who came to Philadelphia with William Penn on his ship the *Welcome*. The company took first prize for its long rectangular shovel at the 1876 Centennial Exhibition in Fairmount Park. (Courtesy of Dennis Lebofsky.)

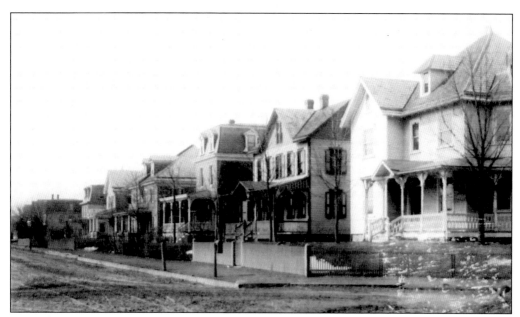

Seen above is a series of homes on Crispin Street, named for the Crispin family. Captain William Crispin of the British navy was William Penn's cousin, who met an untimely death on his way to America in 1681. His son, Silas, and Thomas Holme sailed here in 1682 on the ship *Amity*. Silas's son, Benjamin, became state senator in 1840 and resided in a large property at Welsh Road and Frankford Avenue. (Courtesy of Robert Morris Skaler.)

The Holme Crispin Cemetery is situated on a large plot of land along Holme Avenue, southeast of its intersection with Roosevelt Boulevard. The stone marker shown here was installed in 1863 by trustees of Lower Dublin Academy to replace an anonymous stone marker. Various Holme and Crispin family members are buried at this location. (Courtesy of Dennis Lebofsky.)

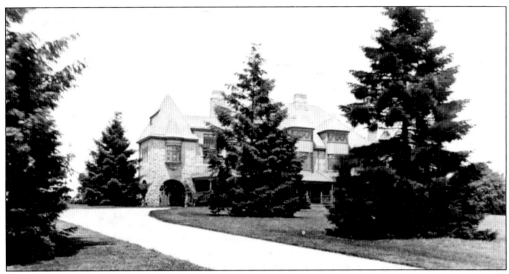

Stonyhurst is an elegant mansion that still stands on Solly Avenue, west of Frankford Avenue. Containing 18 bedrooms and originally the property of Congressman George Castor, the mansion could accommodate many overnight guests. It was later converted for institutional use operated by the Biddle School of Backward Children. Today it serves as home to the Missionary Servants of the Most Blessed Trinity Order.

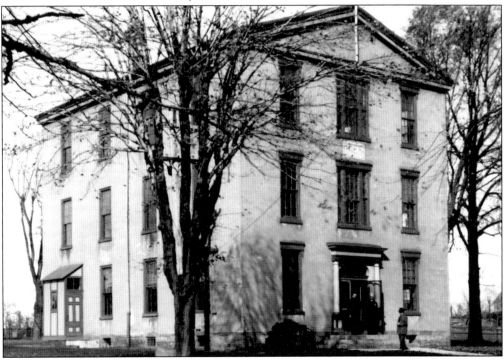

The photograph above, from 1911, depicts the Holmesburg Police Station and local jail, which was situated along Moro Lane, north of Rhawn Street. The building was originally constructed in 1846 as the Columbia Elementary School and remained in use until the Brown School was constructed in 1895. After the station closed, it became a small theater until modern housing was built on what is now Moro Street in the 1950s.

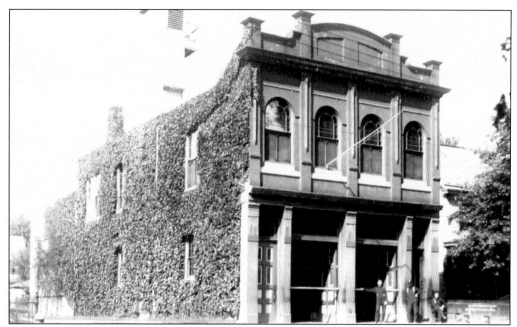

The Holmesburg Firehouse, depicted in the above postcard, was constructed in 1891 and was located at 7818 Frankford Avenue. Ultimately becoming the home of Engine 36 of the Philadelphia Fire Department, the original building was demolished in 1972. A modern fire station was constructed on the site and remains in active use. (Courtesy of Tina Lamb.)

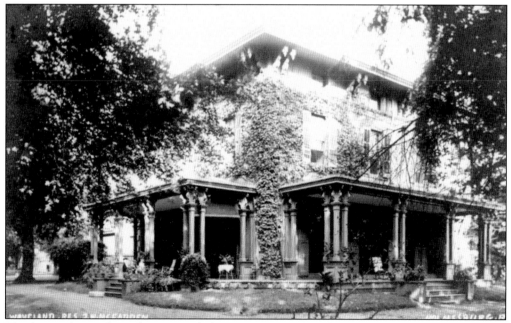

The house depicted on the postcard above was situated at the northeast corner of Frankford Avenue and Ashburner Street. From 1892, the property was owned and occupied for many years by J. W. McFadden, who was the proprietor of a hardware store in Center City Philadelphia. A shopping center occupies most of this site today. (Courtesy of Bruce Conner.)

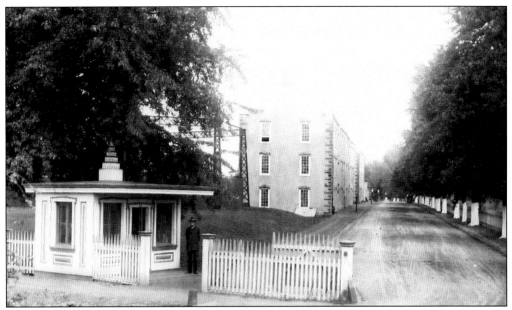

The prison on State Road north of Rhawn Street was built in 1874 and was used to house nonviolent criminals and debtors. It was not until the end of the 19th century that plans were carried out to construct Holmesburg Prison for more hardened offenders. Today this site houses the Curran-Fromhold Correctional Facility. (Courtesy of Dennis Lebofsky.)

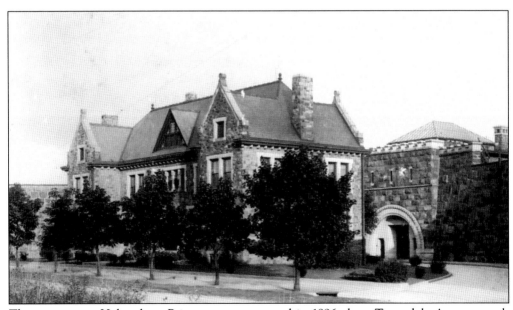

The entrance to Holmesburg Prison was constructed in 1896 along Torresdale Avenue north of Rhawn Street, with fortress-like stone walls around its perimeter. Typical of larger penal institutions from the late 19th century, this facility incorporates spoke-and-wheel architecture with 10 appendages radiating from the center. The prison, which closed in 1995, gained infamy for human medical experimentation in the mid-20th century. (Courtesy of Tina Lamb.)

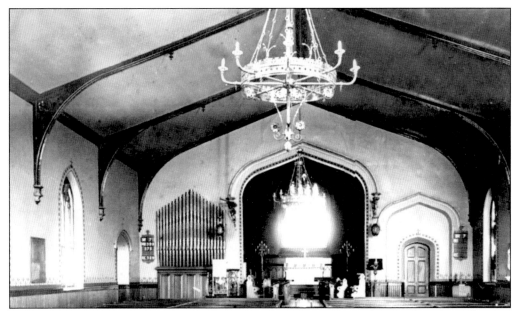

Emmanuel Episcopal Church was founded in 1831 by a congregation that worshiped at All Saints Church. A small chapel was built on land donated by Richard Penn Lardner in 1832. Officially independent of All Saints Church by 1844, by 1858 the congregation was worshiping in the church whose interior is seen above in a postcard from about 1900. (Courtesy of Tina Lamb.)

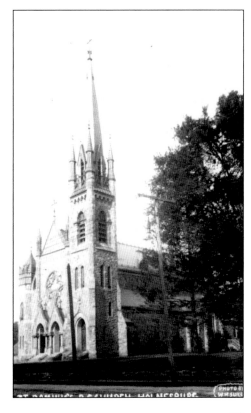

St. Dominic's Roman Catholic Church was built in 1849 and 1850 to serve the needs of a small but growing Catholic population in Holmesburg. Prior to 1850, masses were held in an old stone house by Fr. John Flanagan of Sacred Heart Academy at Eden Hall in Torresdale. A fire in 1897 forced the reconstruction of the church. (Courtesy of Tina Lamb.)

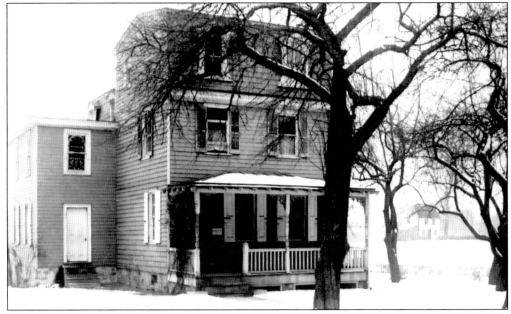

St. Dominic's Roman Catholic Church has its origins in the Murray family home as early as 1847, with an old stone house providing home to an altar that was provided by founder Rev. John Dominic Berrill. A new church building and school were eventually built, along with the convent seen above. A cemetery is located on grounds once occupied by the General Wayne Inn, built in 1718. (Courtesy of Tina Lamb.)

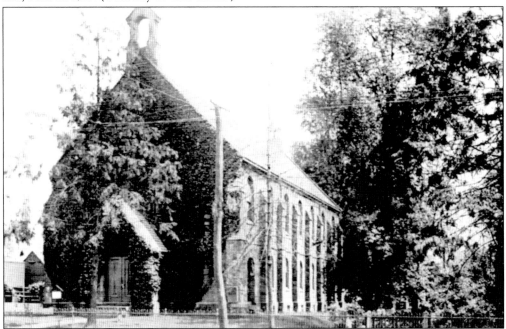

Holmesburg Baptist Church was originally constructed between 1829 and 1831 and has been located south of Rhawn Street at 7927 Frankford Avenue since its founding. It is still in active use today. The original building burned down in 1865 and, in 1867, was reconstructed as seen in this c. 1915 postcard. (Courtesy of Bruce Conner.)

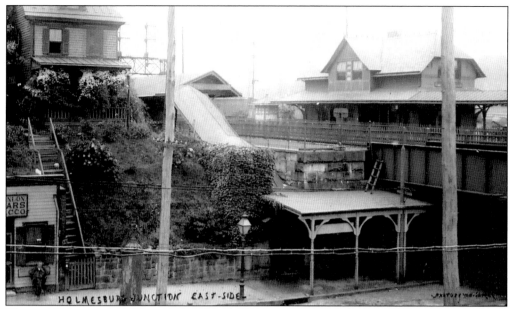

This c. 1900 view shows the ornate assemblage of structures and site improvements that made up the Holmesburg railroad station. Seen from across Rhawn Street on its easterly side, the station featured a Victorian-style railroad and ticket office, decorative wrought-iron fencing, covered walkway and platform, as well as a ground-level cigar and tobacco shop. (Courtesy of Dennis Lebofsky.)

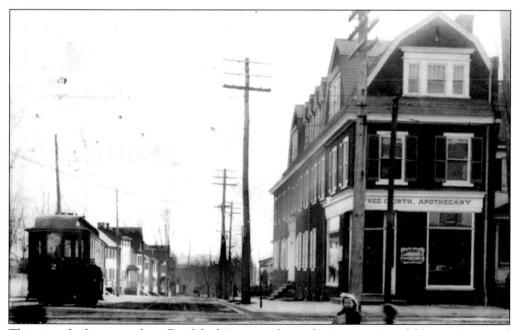

This view, looking east from Frankford Avenue, shows the intersection of Rhawn Street and Frankford Avenue. The building on the right, which still stands, was purchased as a two-story building by druggist Fred C. Orth in 1871. The building was expanded to include a third floor plus a two-story addition along Rhawn Street. (Courtesy of Bruce Conner.)

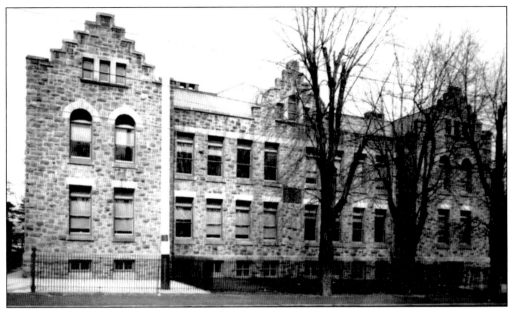

This school building, constructed in 1895, was situated at the southwest corner of Stanwood Street and Frankford Avenue. Named in honor of Joseph Henry Brown (a prominent Holmesburg politician elected to the city council in 1881), this structure was demolished in 1937, along with several structures along Frankford Avenue, to make way for the modern facility that is on the site today. (Courtesy of Tina Lamb.)

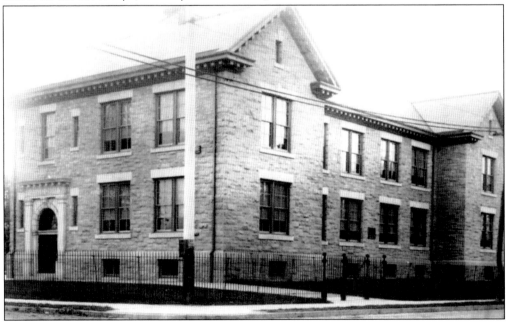

The school building shown here was constructed in 1905 and 1906 and was named in honor of Benjamin Crispin. Situated at the southwest corner of Ditman and Rhawn Streets, it was located in the easterly part of Holmesburg to accommodate a growing population. The school closed in 1983 and was eventually demolished to make way for a new recreation center. (Courtesy of Tina Lamb.)

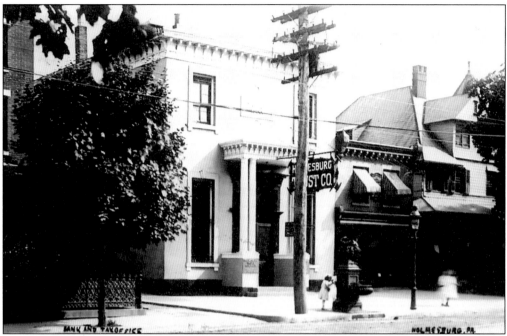

The building at 8041 Frankford Avenue was constructed as the Athenaeum in 1850. Built in the Greek Revival style, it has had many uses, first as a library and reading room, later as Holmesburg Trust Company and headquarters of a local newspaper. Today it is a private enterprise. Next door was the Philadelphia Department of Public Works branch office. (Courtesy of Dennis Lebofsky.)

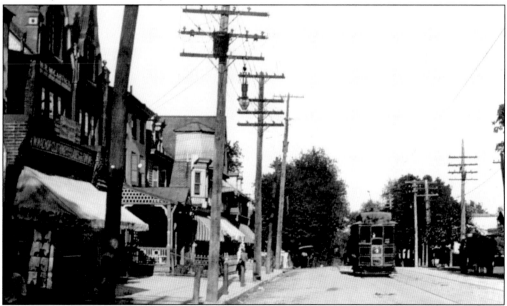

This view looks in a southerly direction along the 8000 block of Frankford Avenue. Seen to the right is the No. 4 trolley of the Holmesburg, Tacony & Frankford Railway Company, affectionately known by locals as the Hop, Toad & Frog line. This line eventually became part of the Philadelphia Transit Company. (Courtesy of Rudy DeFinis.)

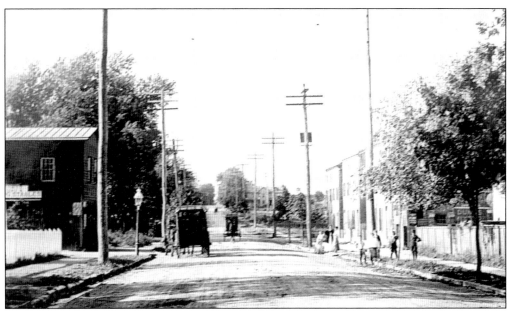

After achieving village status, what is known as Holmesburg was originally known as Washingtonville, in honor of George Washington. As the Holme descendants began selling off land to various individuals and farms, the area grew to be called Holmesburg. Pictured c. 1900 is Rhawn Street, looking west from what is today Frankford Avenue. (Courtesy of Rudy DeFinis.)

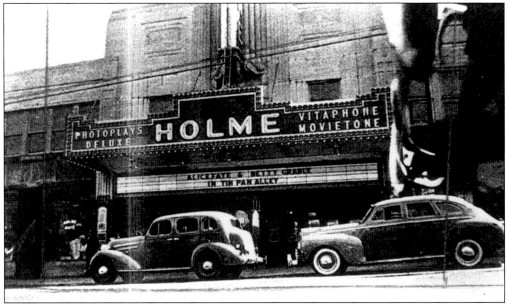

In 1928, the old Washington House was razed to construct a building considered, at the time, to be a testament to the commercial growth of Holmesburg. The Holme Theater cost over $1 million to construct and featured a large, two-story foyer and four attached, bilevel storefronts. In later years, the theater was known as the Penypak. The building still stands today, vacant after years of use as a furniture showroom. (Courtesy of Rudy DeFinis.)

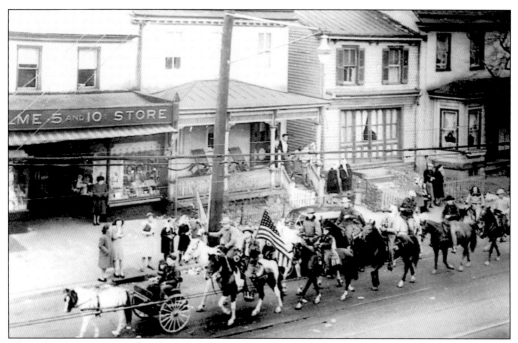

The Thanksgiving parade of 1935 is shown traveling south along the 8000 block of Frankford Avenue. Parades have been staples of proud communities since the late 1800s, and the Mayfair-Holmesburg Parade continues to this day every year around Thanksgiving. Popular stores along this stretch of the avenue at this time included the Holme dime store and Peggy's Sweet Shop. (Courtesy of Rudy DeFinis.)

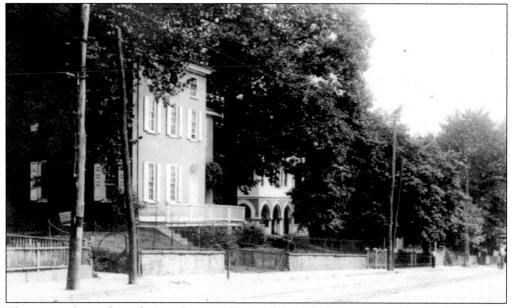

The postcard seen here depicts the 8200 block of Frankford Avenue, south of Solly Avenue, looking in a northerly direction. The building seen in the postcard at one time housed girls who attended the Chapman School, a private boarding school that existed from 1831 to 1875 and was operated by Sara Chapman. (Courtesy of Tina Lamb.)

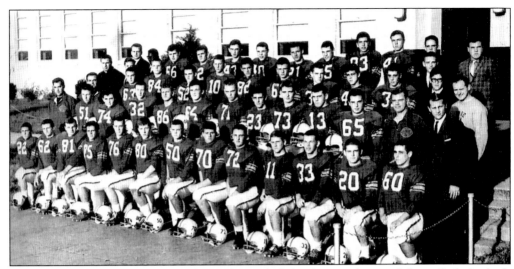

Not long after the construction of Lincoln High School, a need existed for a Catholic high school for boys to serve the booming population of the Lower Northeast. Father Judge High School, whose 1962 football team is seen above, was constructed in the 1950s at Solly and Rowland Avenues to satisfy that need. The school is operated by the Order of St. Francis DeSales. The first class graduated in 1957. (Courtesy of Dennis Lebofsky.)

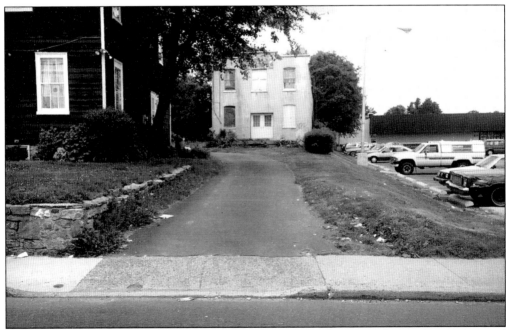

The property at 8712 Frankford Avenue dated from the mid-1800s and over the years served the residents of the area as a livery stable and blacksmith shop. The building was situated just south of the Pathmark supermarket and was demolished in the early 1990s, along with the old residence at the front, to make way for 18 duplexes.

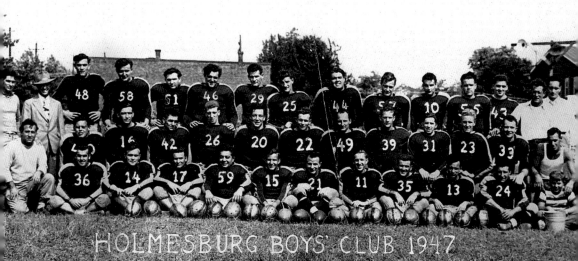

This is the football team of the 1947 Holmesburg Boys' Club. From left to right are the following: (front row) Yockavina (coach), Waltz, Bowen, Hiller, Diasio, J. Robinson, Van Fossen, Clark, Lynn, Benecassa, and Diasio (the water boy); (middle row) Anterola, Walsh, Kupper, J. Cornine, Whitey, McNabb, Nellett, F. Robinson, Dowling, Lowe, McKinski, and Carbona (coach); (back row) Green (coach), Cava (coach), French, Hefferman, Staszak, McNally, Miller, Jarrett, Thompson, Hartwell, Wiggs, Hartman, E. Cornine, Keck (coach), and Coblenz (coach).

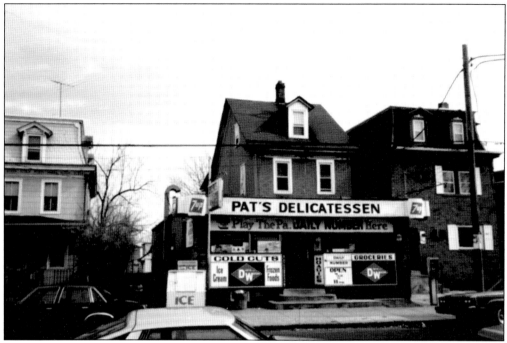

The property pictured in this 1982 photograph is reminiscent of grocery stores from a simpler time and characterizes older neighborhoods such as Holmesburg, Frankford, and Tacony. Once part of the old Unity-Frankford chain of stores and still known today as Pat's Deli, the building is located just west of the intersection of Rhawn and Ditman Streets.

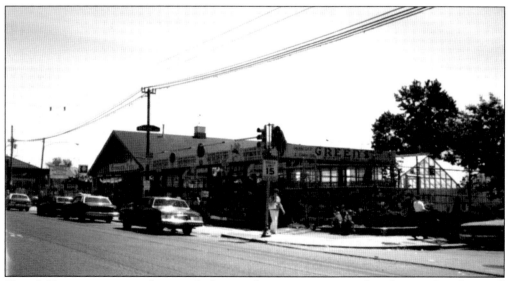

Green's Nursery was a popular spot for buying flowers, greenery, and garden supplies. It served Holmesburg and the surrounding communities for many years along the easterly side of Frankford Avenue, between Strahle and Benson Streets. This property was demolished in the mid-1990s to facilitate development of a CVS Pharmacy.

Three

PENNYPACK

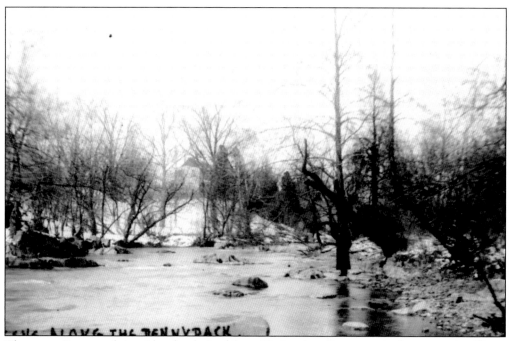

The name Pennypack is said to be derived from Native American terminology meaning "deep, dead water" or "water without much current." Other variations on ancient maps included Dublin Run, since the creek flowed through what was Lower Dublin Township. Seen above is a view along the creek from about 1905. (Courtesy of Tina Lamb.)

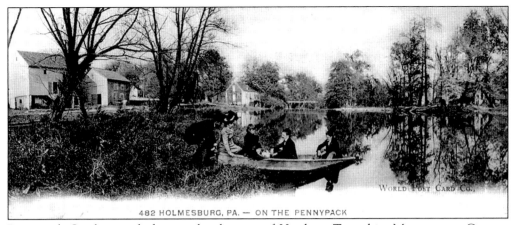

482 HOLMESBURG, PA. — ON THE PENNYPACK

Pennypack Creek extends from its height west of Horsham Township, Montgomery County, a distance of approximately 21 miles as it winds it way to the mouth of the Delaware River in Upper Holmesburg. The linear distance is only 14 miles or so. Seen here is a postcard depicting a recreational outing at Holmesburg. (Courtesy of Bruce Conner.)

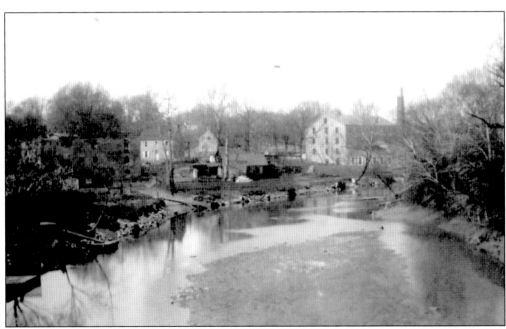

The oldest mill along the creek in the Lower Northeast Philadelphia was situated midway between what is today Torresdale and Frankford Avenues. Philadelphia businessman Charles Saunders and millwright Peter Dale built a gristmill here around 1679. Reportedly more than 70,000 bushels of wheat were manufactured into flour in a given year. The Pennypack Creek is shown in a view looking west from Torresdale Avenue c. 1910. (Courtesy of Bruce Conner.)

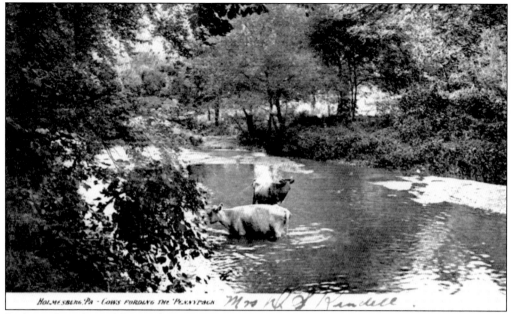

In the earliest days of the northeast section of Philadelphia, the mills that were constructed by the creeks existed alongside mostly farmland. Depicted in the postcard above is an image one may not see along the Pennypack today: wayward cows grazing at the creek. (Courtesy of Tina Lamb.)

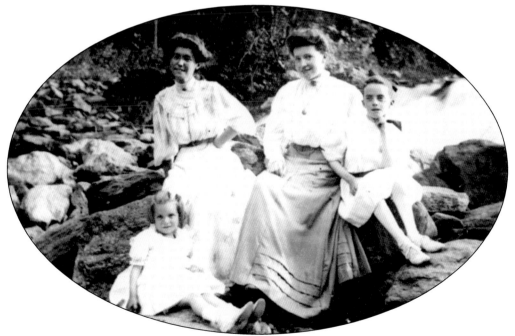

A small group is shown enjoying the serenity of the Pennypack Creek in Holmesburg around 1900. These unidentified subjects, posed on one of the large rocks that provide natural respites from the flow of the creek, display the appropriate fashion of the time for a typical day of recreation. (Courtesy of Dennis Lebofsky.)

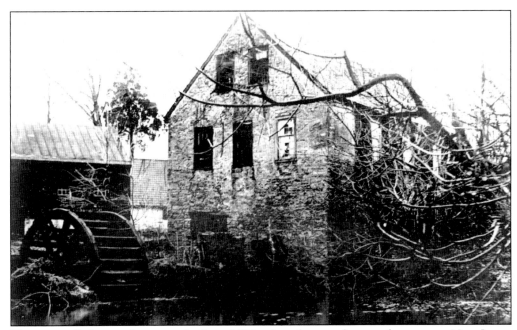

The gristmill shown above was built in 1697, when farmers from as far away as New Jersey would row up the Pennypack Creek to unload grain and return with flour. The mill passed through the hands of John Holme and Robert Lewis before fire destroyed it in 1880. (Courtesy of Bruce Conner.)

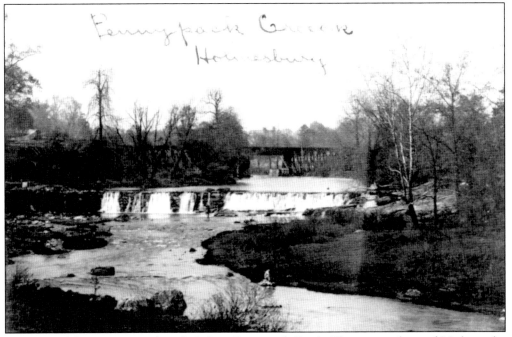

In 1916, 50 fish species were identified along Pennypack Creek. This was made up of 26 above the dams, 4 in ponds or ditches alongside the creek, and 20 in tidal or river regions, including sturgeon some five to six feet long. Many species are no longer in the creek due to pollution and a reduction in the water table. Seen above is a scenic view of the creek. (Courtesy of Tina Lamb.)

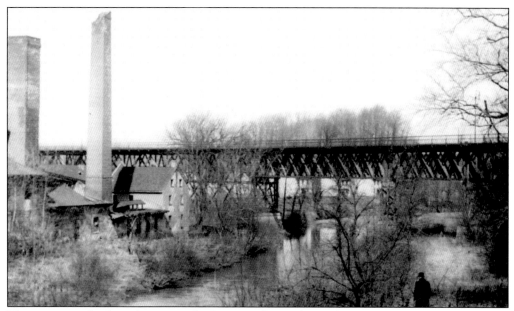

There are two bridges that cross the Pennypack Creek at Rhawn Street. The upper Rhawn Street Bridge is located near Lexington Avenue while the lower bridge, pictured here c. 1905, is located west of Rowland Avenue. Seen above is the old lower Rhawn Street Bridge before the wooden structure was replaced by concrete around 1920. To the left are the ruins of the Pennypack Print Works. (Courtesy of Robert Morris Skaler.)

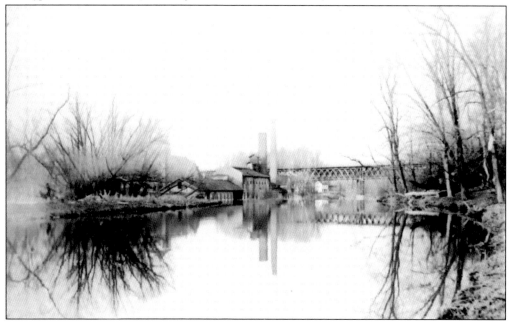

Samuel Comly built these printworks (used for dying cloth) in an old mill near the lower Rhawn Street bridge. It was named the Pennypack Print Works in 1939 by the successive owner, Joseph Ripka. Many of its workers lived in cottages on low-lying land next to the printworks. The mill was powered entirely by waterpower and was rendered obsolete after the advent of the steam engine. (Courtesy of Robert Morris Skaler.)

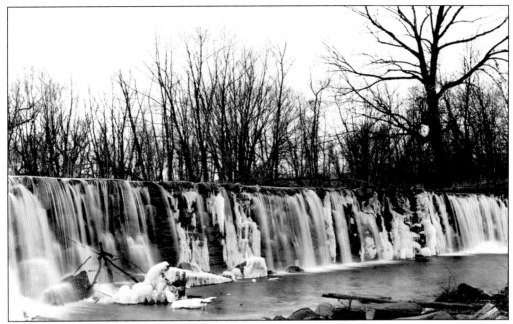

This 1921 photograph shows a partially frozen Pennypack Creek waterfall near the lower Rhawn Street bridge. In the 1930s, the New Deal's Civil Works Administration and Works Progress Administration resulted in far-reaching public improvements to the park, including 20 miles of bridle paths and recreational areas for swimming.

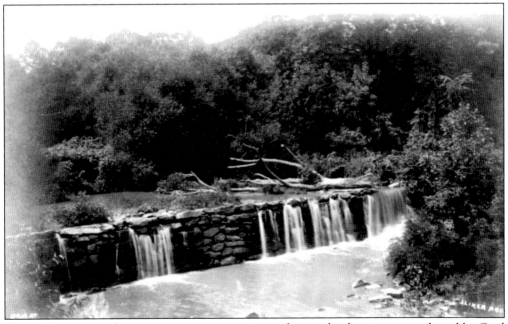

Crystal Springs was the name given to a mansion and grounds when it was purchased by Civil War hero Col. James Lewis in 1883. The property was built in 1855 and was located on the Pennypack Creek near Rhawn and Rowland Avenues. It had been used for a time as a hotel or bed and breakfast, and the spring on the property was famous for its clear water. Shown here is the dam at Crystal Springs c. 1910. (Courtesy of Bruce Conner.)

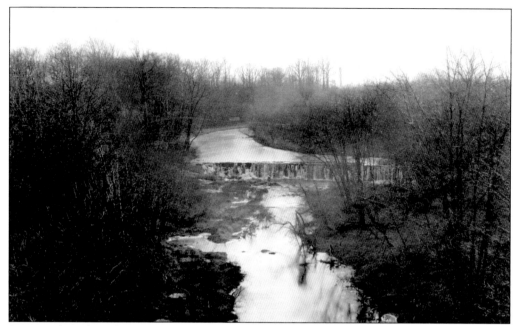

Pennypack Park and Creek in winter can be sights to behold, and views starkly contrast with the dense greenery of spring and summer. Over 40 bird species were identified on a typical winter's day around 1960, including various hawks, sparrows, woodpeckers, and crows. Seen above in the winter of 1921 is the dam near what used to be Crystal Springs.

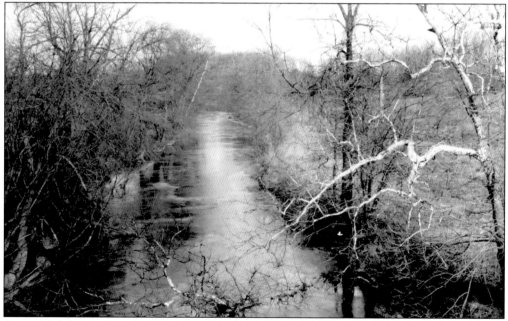

Animal life has been and continues to be abundant in areas along the Pennypack Creek. Deer are more plentiful in westerly portions of the Pennypack, and the occasional beaver and weasel have been observed. Other more common inhabitants include red fox, raccoon, squirrels, chipmunks, muskrats, rabbit, and a variety of snakes, toads, frogs, salamanders, and turtles. Seen above is a creek view north from the upper Rhawn Street bridge in 1921.

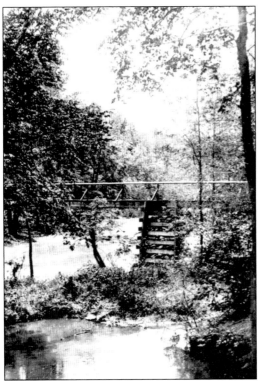

A list compiled in the early 1960s counted a total of 256 bird species populating the areas along the Pennypack Creek. The highest bird count in a single day was reportedly 119 varieties in the spring of 1943. Seen here is a picturesque postcard view of a wooden footbridge along the creek at Holmesburg.

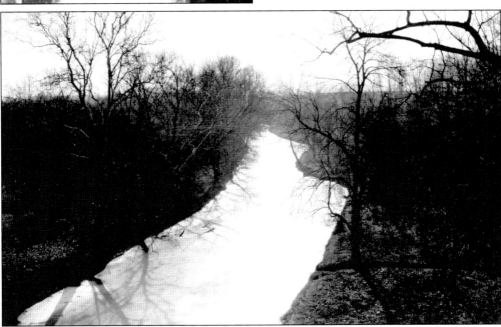

An extensive study in the 1950s observed many varieties of trees along the creek. Sweet gum and paulownia were found, as well as some exotic species like arbor vitae and crab apple along westerly portions of the creek. Other common varieties included silver maple, Norway spruce, tulip, willow, beech, and red, black, and white oak. Seen above is a creek view south from the Holme Avenue bridge in 1921.

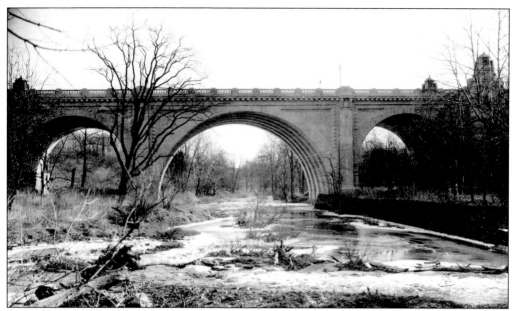

Seen above is the creek as it flows under the Bensalem Avenue bridge at Roosevelt Boulevard, which was completed in 1920 and engineered by Day and Zimmerman. At the time, the boulevard extended like spokes to Poquessing Avenue, Holme Avenue, and Bensalem Avenue, which eventually became the main route of the new Lincoln Highway to New York and part of the boulevard.

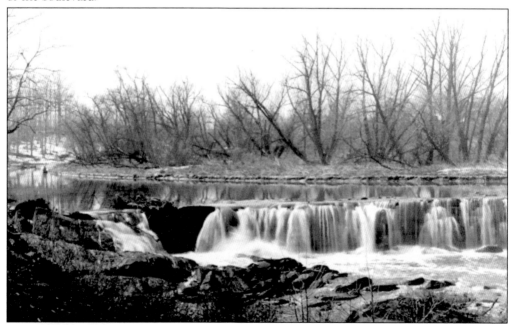

Friends of Pennypack Park, established as Friends of the Pennypack in 1953, was created to oversee improvements and maintenance of the park and creek in conjunction with the Fairmount Park Commission. Over 50 years later, the park remains an urban oasis of natural beauty due to the efforts of this civic-minded body. Seen above is a small waterfall on the creek c. 1915. (Courtesy of Bruce Conner.)

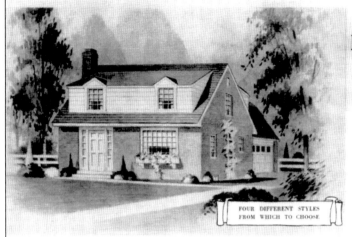

Winchester Park

Adjoining PENNYPACK PARK *and* MAYFAIR

Winchester Park is almost surrounded by Pennypack Park, providing over a mile of Park frontage. Although adjoining Mayfair, Pennypack Park serves as a barrier preventing the row-type dwellings from growing up to it, thus preserving permanently the suburban atmosphere of the community and the value of the homes built here.

FOUR DIFFERENT STYLES FROM WHICH TO CHOOSE

"RECIPE FOR SHANGRI-LA LIVING"

Winchester Park is a planned postwar community conceived to provide suburban living, contrasting with the row dwellings springing up in adjacent Mayfair. The advertisement seen above boasts a "recipe for Shangri-La living" with over a mile of Pennypack Park frontage and 31 miles of picturesque bridle paths, without the cost of upkeep. The ad goes on to state, "Kiddies will grow robust and strong in this wonderful, healthful environment."

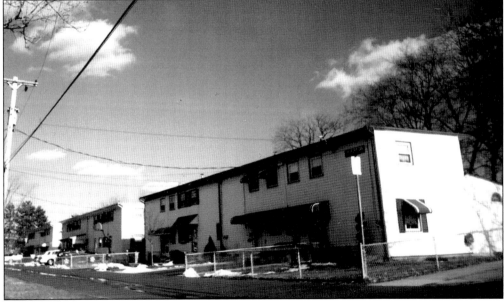

Pennypack Woods was a government-sponsored cooperative community, one of eight built between 1940 and 1945, which was turned over to its residents at the end of World War II. This community sprung up on 120 acres between Holme Avenue and Frankford Avenue. Seen above is a typical street within the community, whose homeowners association adheres to strict policies in order to maintain a stable and healthful environment.

Four

TORRESDALE

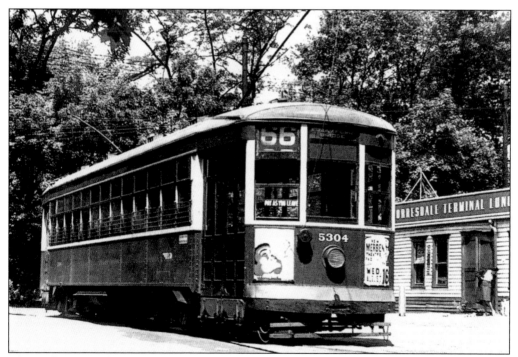

The trolley seen above is the Route 66 line making its way back south around the curve at the city limits near Knights Road. The luncheonette seen to the right is still standing and for decades has been in use as a bar. Note the poster on the front of the trolley for the new Merben Theatre in Mayfair. (Courtesy of Rudy DeFinis.)

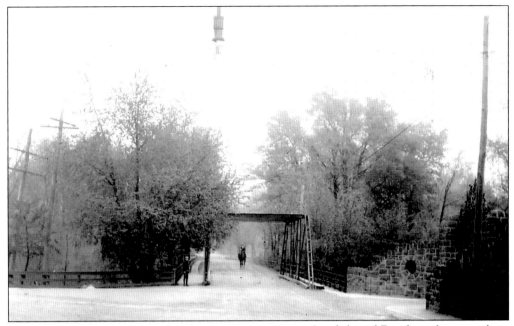

Torresdale's first inhabitants after the Lenni Lenape were Swedish and Dutch settlements along the Delaware River. Evan Thomas occupied one of the first notable riverfront properties known as the Bake House. Thomas is said to have baked bread for George Washington's troops during the American Revolution. His bakery served cargo ships that would use his wharf. Seen above is State Road looking north over the Poquessing Creek bridge. (Courtesy of Dennis Lebofsky.)

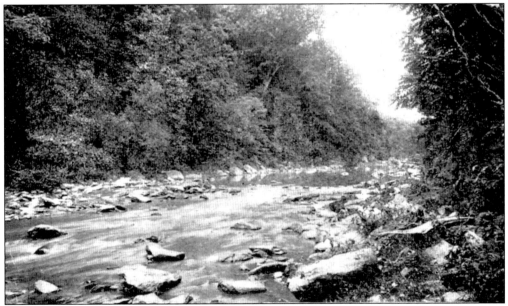

Torresdale was the name chosen for the village of approximately 670 acres founded where the Poquessing Creek, seen above, meets the Delaware River. Torresdale was the town in Scotland from which the ancestors of Charles Macalester hailed. In 1850, Macalester, an influential banker and American diplomat, purchased a lot on the river, built a home he called Glengarry, and named the area after that of his forefathers.

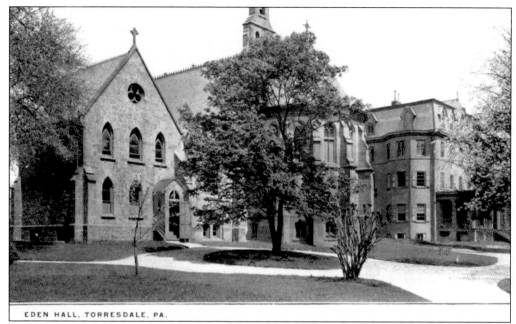

EDEN HALL, TORRESDALE, PA.

Eden Hall was originally purchased by the Sisters of the Sacred Heart to build a boarding school for girls. A chapel was built that still stands today on dedicated grounds, known as Fluehr Park and maintained by the Fairmount Park Commission. A detached single-family residential development called Eden Hall occupies part of the site today.

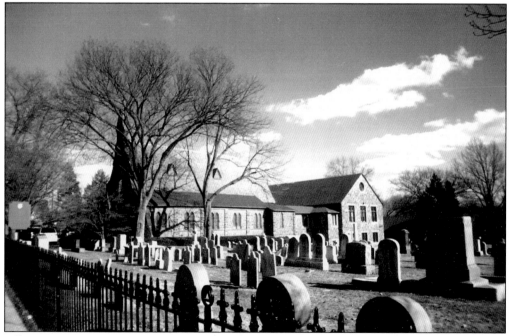

All Saints Episcopal Church was originally constructed in 1773 and is one of the oldest churches still active in Philadelphia. The stone church seen above is situated along the easterly side of Frankford Avenue, south of Grant Avenue. In the old days, the building was also used as a meeting place.

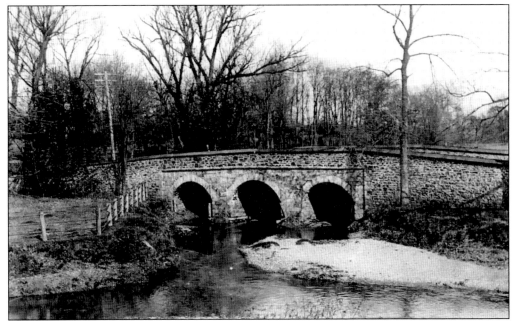

The Poquessing Creek was named for the Lenni Lenape village named Peetquesink, which was established along its banks. Two of the original landowners before Charles Macalester were Swedes by the names of Olle Coeckal and Lars Larson. The postcard above depicts the bridge over the creek at Frankford Avenue from the city limits. (Courtesy of Bruce Conner.)

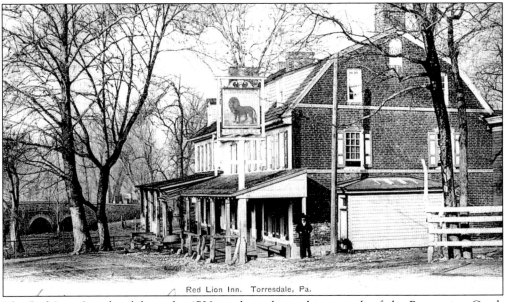

Red Lion Inn. Torresdale, Pa.

The Red Lion Inn dated from the 1730s and was located just north of the Poquessing Creek along the old King's Highway from Torresdale and the city of Philadelphia. It is said that in 1781, George Washington and his troops camped for the night in fields adjacent to the inn on their way to Virginia from New York. The building was destroyed by fire in the 1980s.

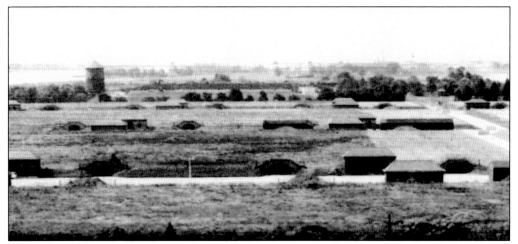

In 1909, the Torresdale filter plant, seen above, was constructed along the banks of the Delaware River between Pennypack Street and Linden Avenue. Utilizing underground sand filters, the plant supplied clean water for a substantial part of the city's population. About 50 years later, the plant was replaced by a more modern facility in order to keep up with growing demand and make more efficient its pre-treatment and post-treatment facilities.

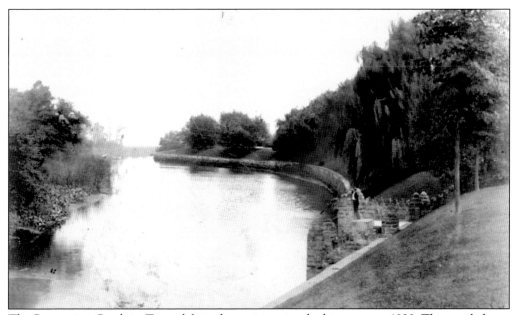

The Poquessing Creek in Torresdale is shown in a view looking west c. 1920. This creek forms the northerly boundary of the city of Philadelphia, with Bucks County situated across the Poquessing. Relics of the Lenni Lenape presence are occasionally unearthed along the creek, where forts and trading posts were located long ago. (Courtesy of Robert Morris Skaler.)

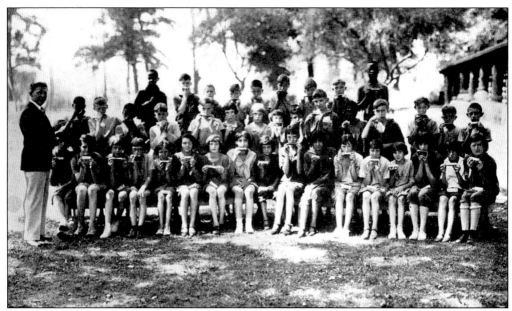

Camp Happy, located at Linden Avenue and Torresdale Avenue, was a city-owned day camp for underprivileged children. The site is part of a Philadelphia Department of Recreation center today. The above photograph, taken in 1925, depicts attendees who were part of the harmonica band, with the director seen at the far left.

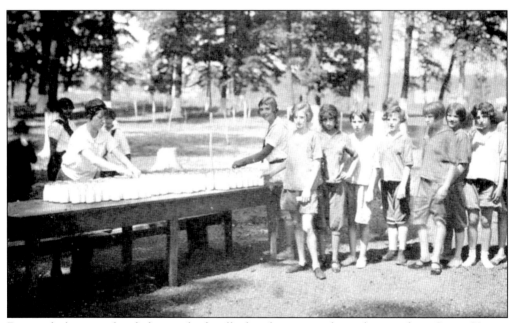

Depicted above is the daily ritual of milk distribution to the girls attending Camp Happy. Viewed as a model of public day camps, the facility featured a recreational log cabin, playground with carousel, flower garden, swimming pool, infirmary, mess hall, and tennis and volleyball courts. Tents were erected in separate boys' and girls' sections, and activities included morning and evening patriotic exercises.

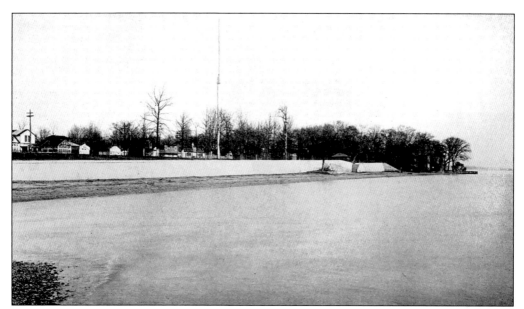

Pleasant Hill Bathing Beach, seen above, was a popular recreational spot in the early part of the 20th century. In the mid-1920s, the city of Philadelphia created a retaining wall topped with wrought-iron fencing and an outdoor shower with turnstile entry, picnic grounds, anchorage for canoes, parking area, two baseball diamonds, and six tennis courts. A 1925 municipal report called Pleasant Hill one of the finest bathing beaches in the country.

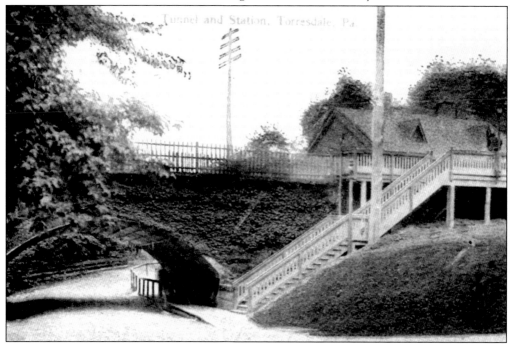

Grant Avenue is one of Torresdale's main east–west thoroughfares and was probably named for Samuel Grant, one of the first purchasers of land out of the holdings of Charles Macalester. Seen above in a postcard that dates from about 1915 is Grant Avenue near its intersection with James Street, just west of the Torresdale railroad station.

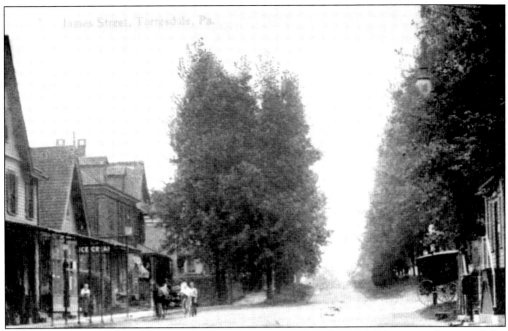

James Street south of Grant Avenue is shown when it was the main shopping district of the village of Torresdale. A barbershop, drugstore, and grocery store with delivery by horse and wagon all lined this street, now occupied by various residential and light commercial users. The site of the old Torresdale Post Office now serves as a parking lot for Septa's Torresdale rail station. (Courtesy of Bruce Conner.)

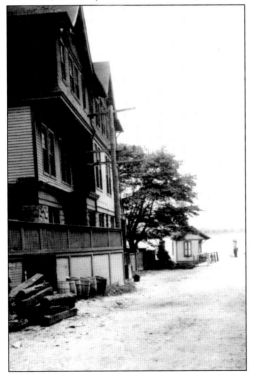

The Torresdale Wharf was notorious as one of the most plentiful spots for catching shad at the beginning of the 20th century. Bustling with activity during shad season, the wharf served as the collecting site for shipment to central Philadelphia on fast steamships. Seen c. 1910 is the boat landing at Linden Avenue. (Courtesy of Bruce Conner.)

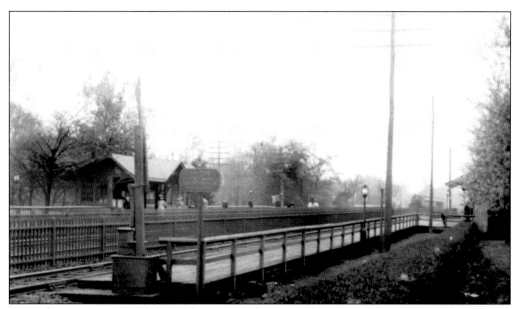

Seen above is a postcard from about 1915 depicting the Torresdale station and tracks. In the early part of the 20th century, fish from the state hatcheries, which were at Linden and Delaware Avenues, were loaded daily on horse and wagon to be shipped throughout the state from the Torresdale station. (Courtesy of Bruce Conner.)

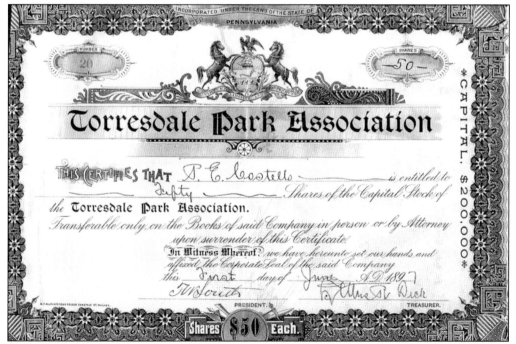

This stock certificate was issued to builder and politician Peter E. Costello on June 1, 1897. The amusement park operated near Frankford Avenue and Knights Road from about 1880. An 1897 dispute between the park's operator, Robert A. Rockhill, and the Torresdale Park Association preceded its ultimate closure in 1906. The dispute was over the retention by the park of refreshment booths and ice-cream and candy pavilions upon the expiration of his lease in 1896.

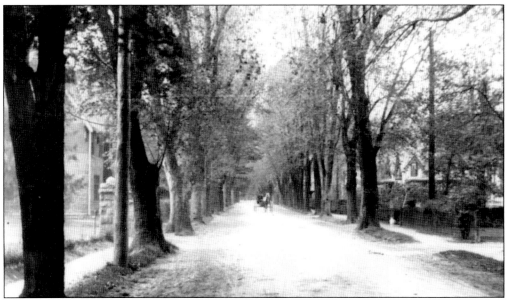

Seen above is Milnor Street looking south *c*. 1915. The area between State Road, the Delaware River, Grant Avenue, and Fitler Street was known as Resort Town. The private home at Grant Avenue and Wissinoming Street was reportedly operated as a casino. Torresdale's riverfront was one of the last areas to retain its recreational and residential appeal after institutional and industrial uses took over most of the riverfront by 1905. (Courtesy of Bruce Conner.)

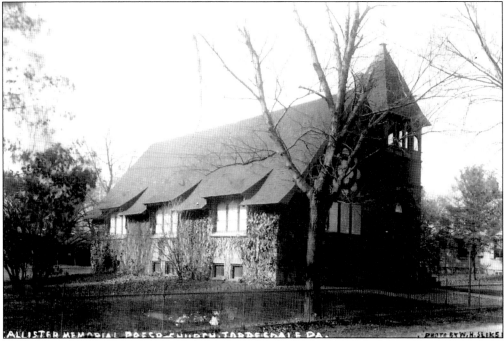

The stone edifice in this postcard from about 1910 is the Macalester Memorial Presbyterian Church, which was built by Torresdale's founder Charles Macalester. It was situated along Grant Avenue east of State Road. This church was eventually demolished and the facility moved to a site on Morrell Avenue. (Courtesy of Dennis Lebofsky.)

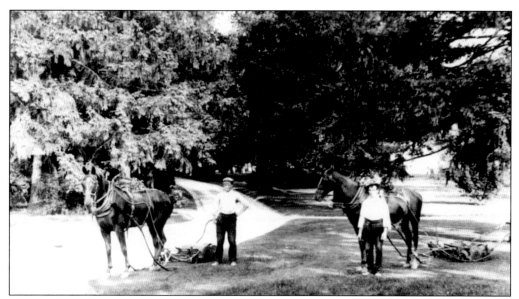

Charles Macalester's Glengarry Estate was eventually purchased by Robert H. Foerderer, who admired the property since rowing past at the age of 19. He made his fortune in the leather business. Foerderer made substantial additions to the home, including a large enclosed porch and massive dining room. He changed the estate's name to Glen Foerd, bridging together the original estates by combining the two names. Seen above are Foerderer's grounds c. 1910. (Courtesy of Bruce Conner.)

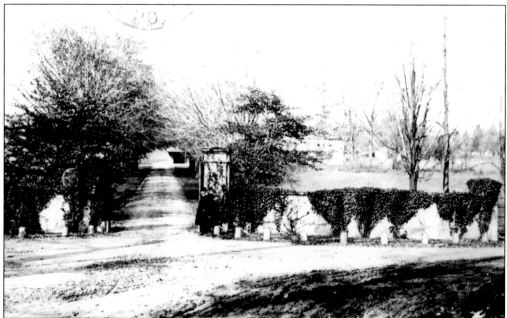

Edward Deveaux Morrell was a lawyer and a colonel in the First City Troop Cavalry of Philadelphia. He was a major landowner in Torresdale's early days. His holdings included the Morelton Inn, a mansion that served to entertain and house acquaintances and friends in the summer months. Seen above is the entrance to Morrell's home, near what is Morrell and Frankford Avenue today. (Courtesy of Dennis Lebofsky.)

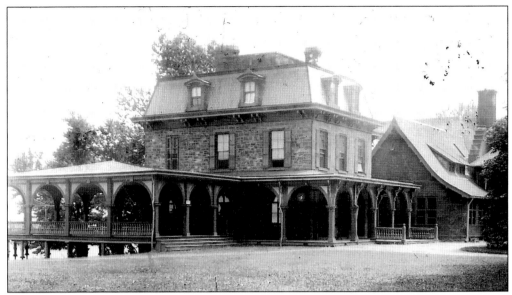

Seen above is Morelton Inn on grounds now occupied by Baker's Bay Condominium development. This property, used as a summer retreat by wealthy Philadelphia area families, featured a casino, tennis courts, and croquet and archery grounds, as well as the finest Victorian landscaping. This property spawned a wave of similar uses at adjacent properties. In later years, it was used by the Delaware River Yacht Club and Home for Aged and Infirm Deaf. (Courtesy of Dennis Lebofsky.)

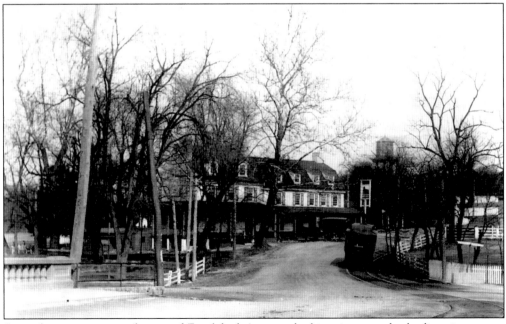

Seen above is a postcard view of Frankford Avenue, looking in a northerly direction across the bridge over Poquessing Creek toward Andalusia, an old village within the township of Bensalem in Bucks County. Note the Red Lion Inn in the distance. Dr. Benjamin Rush, a signer of the Declaration of Independence and one of Torresdale's most notable residents, was born west of here in Torresdale along Red Lion Road. (Courtesy of Bruce Conner.)

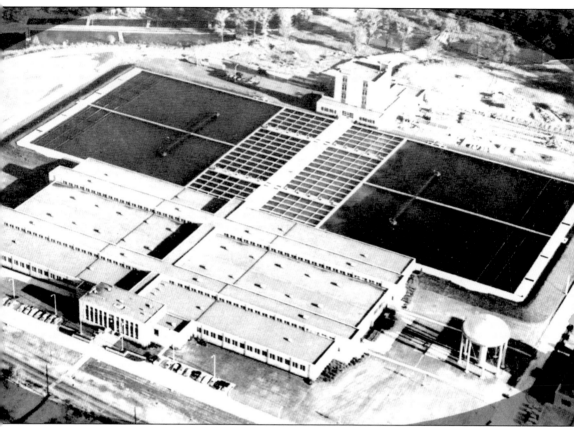

In the 1950s, the Philadelphia Water Department embarked on what was considered one of the most imaginative tasks ever accomplished by the water industry. On just 10 of the 60 acres the original plant occupied at the Delaware River and Pennypack Street, this $25 million facility consists of a one-story filter building with a two-story laboratory and office section along State Road, a five-story preliminary treatment building, a four-story post-treatment building, four outdoor mixing basins, and four outdoor sedimentation basins. In the main building, 94 rapid sand-filter beds were installed. These filters could be operated either manually or automatically and allowed continuity of production, since the individual filter beds were easier to clean than those in the old plant.

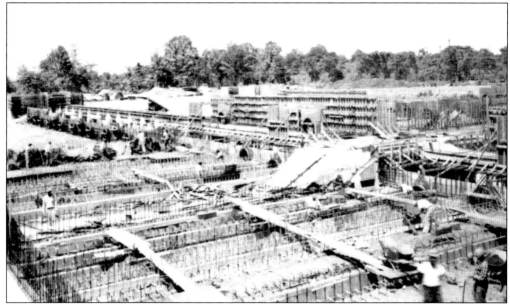

The building of the state-of-the-art Torresdale push-button water-treatment plant, seen above during its construction, required more than 9,000 tons of structural steel, 81,000 cubic yards of concrete, 1.5 million bricks, 268,000 glazed tiles, 130,000 square feet of plaster, and 8,000 cubic yards of drainage stone. The plant was eventually named for Samuel S. Baxter, water commissioner at the time of construction.

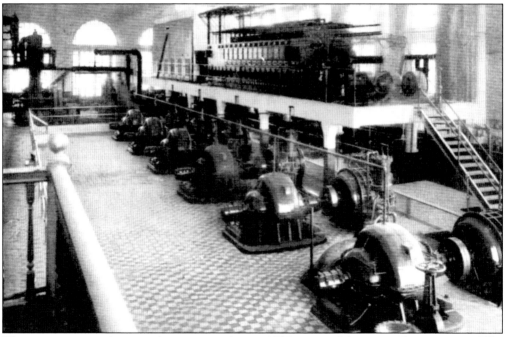

This image appeared in an advertisement from a 1930s issue of *American City* magazine. The ad depicts the interior of the Torresdale Pumping Station and cites the facility as an example of the efficiency provided by Fairbanks-Morse diesel engines. Six centrifugal pumps, each driven by 600-horsepower motors, could handle a capacity of 300 million gallons of water per day.

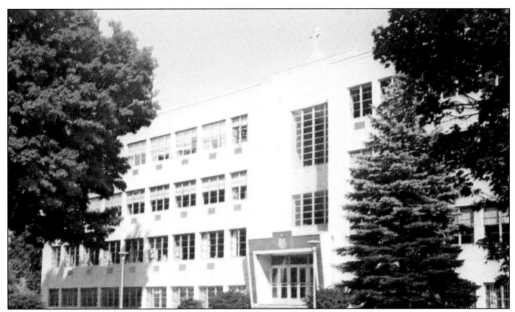

The community of Torresdale has retained its character as one of the most desirable Philadelphia neighborhoods for residential living and continues to be characterized by a harmonious blend of institutional, residential, and commercial uses. Seen above is the main academic building of Holy Family University, dedicated in 1955 and located along the easterly side of Frankford Avenue, north of Grant Avenue. (Courtesy of Dennis Lebofsky.)

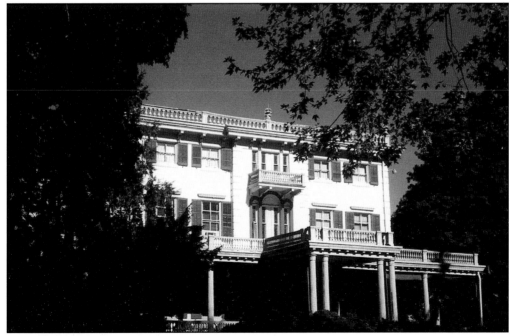

Glen Foerd on the Delaware is the restored building and grounds first known as Glengarry and later enhanced by Robert Foerderer. Today, the property is the site of historic tours, weddings, and special events. The main building, seen above, as well as the outbuildings, vineyard, and garden, take visitors back 100 years to the splendor of the Victorian era.

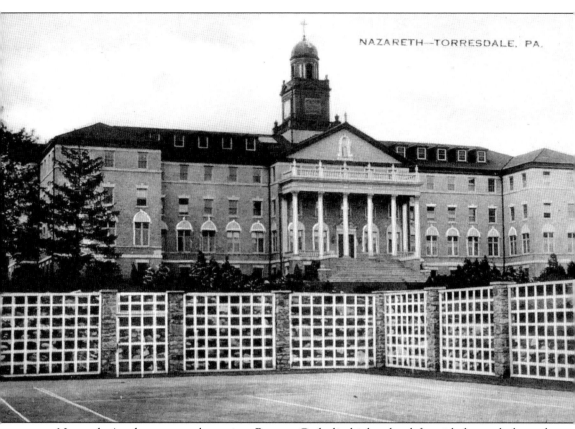

NAZARETH—TORRESDALE, PA.

Nazareth Academy, seen above, is a Roman Catholic high school for girls located along the northerly side of Grant Avenue, west of James Street. Founded in 1928 by Mother M. Idalia of the Sisters of the Holy Family of Nazareth, the academy seeks to foster a living faith to teach the message of Christ, to build community, and to serve humankind. A gymnasium and cafeteria were added to the facility in 1954.

Five

TACONY

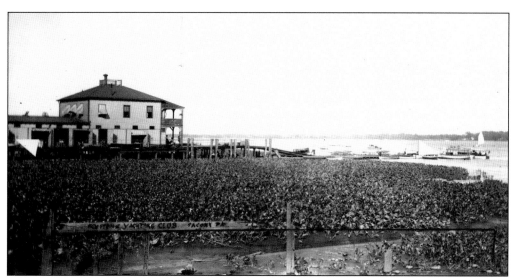

The Keystone Yacht Club, located just north of Princeton Avenue, is shown c. 1910. The Delaware River is on the right. Despite the density of industrial development that sprung up around them, the club (known today as Quaker City Yacht Club) and adjacent St. Vincent's Orphanage property are lingering reminders of the days when recreational and residential uses dominated Tacony's riverfront.

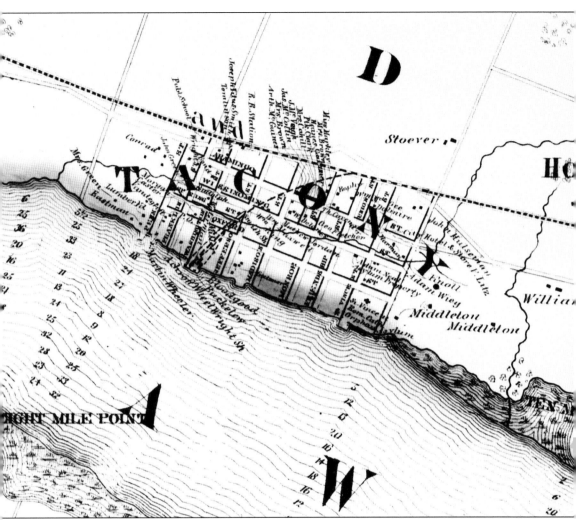

The map pictured above shows Tacony in 1862, about a decade prior to the arrival of Henry Disston. A village sprung up around the rail line secured by William H. Gatzmer, who built his residence on the Delaware River. St. Vincent's Orphanage and Church was built just north of Gatzmer's property. Only a sliver of this original village and St. Vincent's remain today—mostly along Wissinoming Street and State Road (Aramingo Avenue on map)—due to two major phases of redevelopment. The Industrial Revolution in the 19th century brought about major shifts in land use, and the construction of Interstate 95 in the 20th century led to a proliferation of industrial and automotive uses in this area. The lumberyard and the Green and Eastman properties were initial purchases in what amounted to 390 acres of contiguous land holdings for Henry Disston. (Courtesy of Waldo Tulk.)

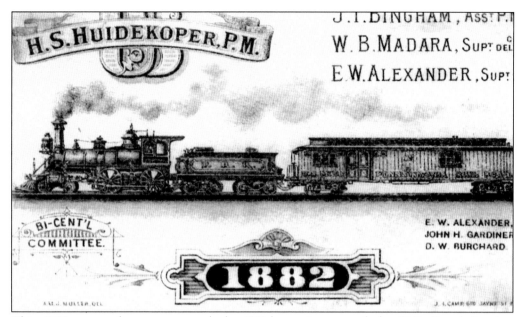

This 1882 postcard commemorated the 200th anniversary of the U.S. Postal Service, referencing the postmaster at the time of issuance and depicting a locomotive to represent the mode of choice for mail delivery at the time. Tacony was the location of the first post office as specifically directed by William Penn, and the area's name was shortened over the years from the Lenni Lenape Towacawoninck, meaning "wilderness."

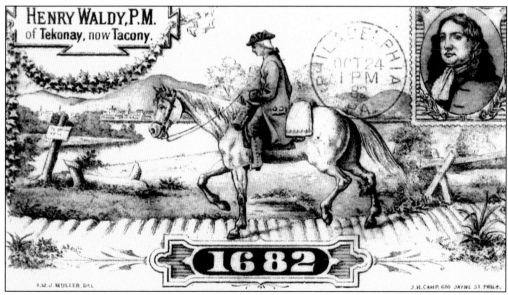

The flipside of the bicentennial commemorative postcard depicts Henry Waldy, the first postmaster under William Penn. He is shown riding a horse along what is likely Plank Road, which paralleled the Delaware River through communities like Bridesburg and Tacony. Note the former spelling of Tacony as "Tekonay."

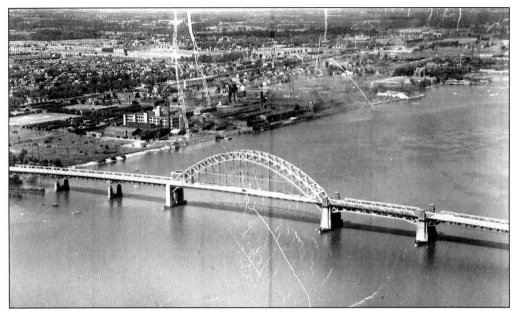

The Tacony-Palmyra Bridge is shown just a few years after it was constructed in 1929. On the left is the ball field and factory of Henry Disston & Sons, which moved its operations from Laurel Street over a quarter-century period from 1872. Henry Disston developed lots out of his tract west of the railroad and made houses available for rent or sale to his employees. (Courtesy of Donna Dizierza, photograph by Frank Wilding.)

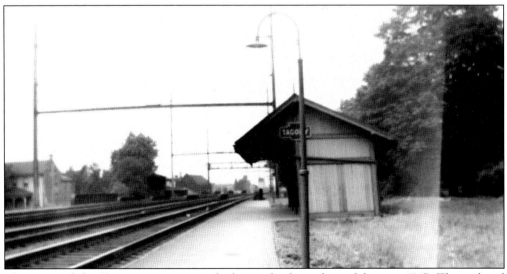

This view of the Tacony train station looks south along the rail line in 1947. The railroad marked the easterly boundary of the Henry Disston estate, as surveyed and laid out into lots in 1885. Disston imposed deed restrictions to prohibit what were considered offensive land uses such as glue-boiling factories, livery stables, and buildings used for the sale and manufacture of alcoholic beverages.

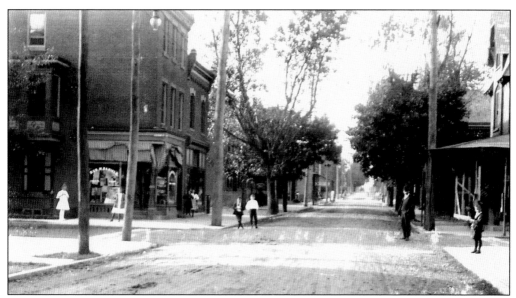

Seen above is an old-time view looking west up Longshore Avenue from Hegerman Street, near the center of the Disston Estate. Longshore Avenue was the commercial center of Tacony until Torresdale Avenue got the trolley in 1906. Henry Disston's deed restrictions are imposed on a 350-acre residential tract, which extends south nearly to Magee Avenue, north to Tyson Avenue (nearly to Princeton Avenue east of Torresdale Avenue), and west to about Cottage Street. (Courtesy of Dennis Lebofsky.)

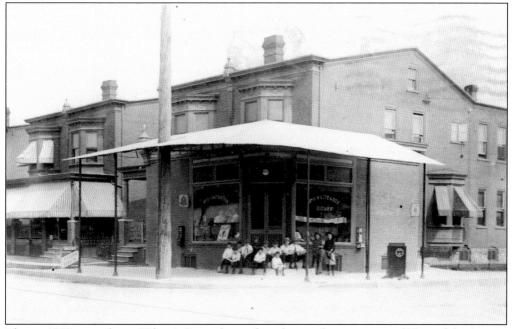

This c. 1910 view shows White's Store, located at the northeast corner of Torresdale Avenue and Unruh Street. This cigar and candy store offered modern conveniences like two wall-mounted pay telephones and a metal canopy over the entryway. Seeking shelter under the canopy is a group of Tacony youths. (Courtesy of Bruce Conner.)

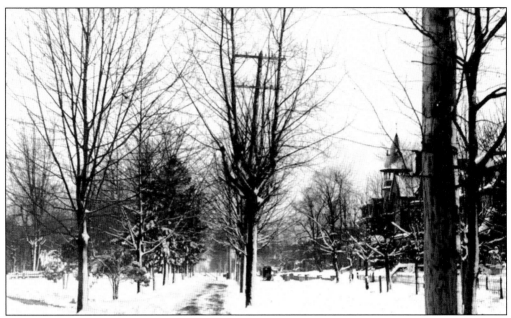

The image depicted above, from a postcard issued c. 1900, shows a picturesque view of a snow-covered Keystone Street looking in a southerly direction from about Tyson Avenue. On the left is Disston Park, a linear park extending along the railroad line, with the largest detached houses of the time lining Keystone Street on the right.

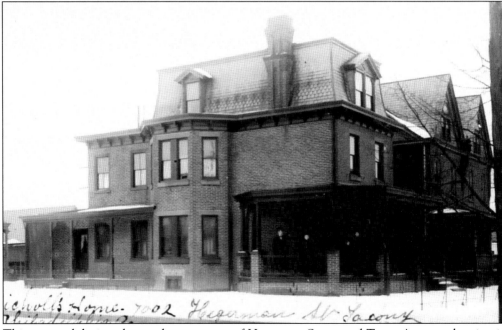

This postcard depicts the northwest corner of Hegerman Street and Tyson Avenue, showing it as the one-time home of the Nicholl family. This block of detached single and semidetached twin homes is characteristic of the heterogeneous blend of residential living styles envisioned when Henry Disston and his sons laid out the original town of Tacony. This block remains virtually intact today, despite some facade alterations. (Courtesy of Bruce Conner.)

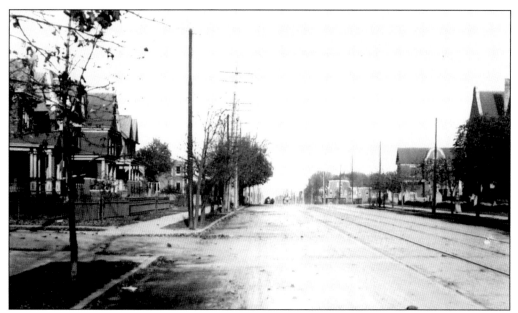

This postcard offers a glimpse of Torresdale Avenue before the wave of commercial development, brought on by the installation of the trolley tracks, took hold. The residences on the right still remain today. However, with the exception of the old Titus Funeral Home (now Disston Manor), the homes and wrought-iron fences on the left were demolished to make way for storefronts with upper-level apartments. (Courtesy of Robert Morris Skaler.)

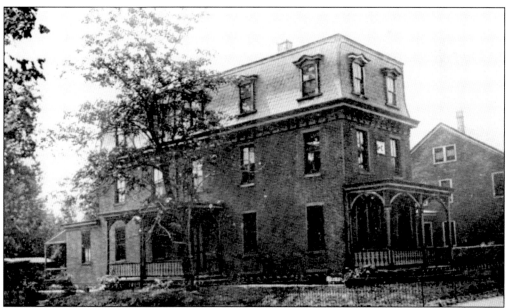

Pictured is the home of the St. Leo Council of the Knights of Columbus, situated at the southeast corner of Tulip Street and Tyson Avenue. Although the facade of the building has changed, its occupant has been the same for about a century. The council is famous locally for their annual food-basket giveaways during the holidays. (Courtesy of Bruce Conner.)

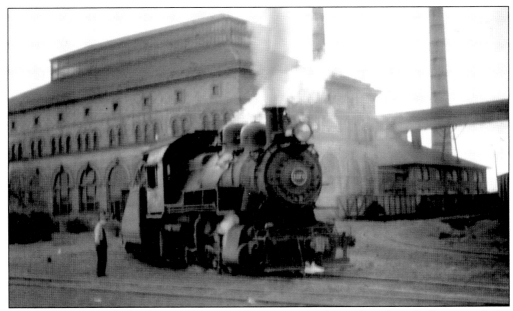

The building seen behind an 1876 steam locomotive is located at Levick Street and the Delaware River and is part of the Lardner's Point Pumping Station. This facility was built in 1904 to generate the force needed to move the city's water to residences and businesses. Water treated at the Torresdale Filter Plant was fed to this station via concrete conduit to the pumping engines housed on the interior. (Courtesy of George Pricskett.)

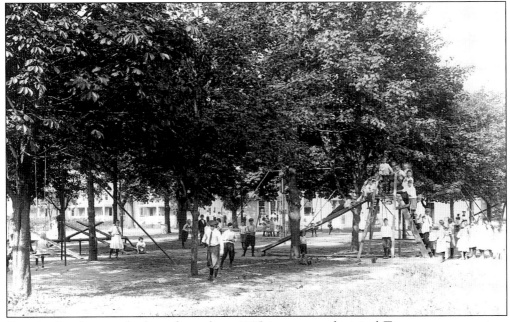

Seen in the photograph above from about 1905 is a group of spirited Tacony youngsters in a playground at an unknown location. Remaining true to Henry Disston's vision of a working-class community with ample open space, the community is dotted with parks and playgrounds like Dorsey, Disston, Roosevelt, and Mullin, with American Legion Playground across the southerly boundary and Russo Park across the northerly boundary at Torresdale Avenue.

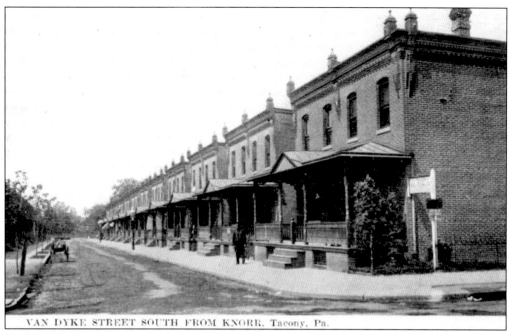

The caption on this postcard incorrectly identifies the view as Vandike Street looking south from Knorr Street, when actually the street scene looks south from Unruh Avenue, one block away. This part of the Disston estate is characterized by smaller row-style and twin residences, which had smaller yards and were built for the typical Disston laborer in Tacony's earliest days. (Courtesy of Bruce Conner.)

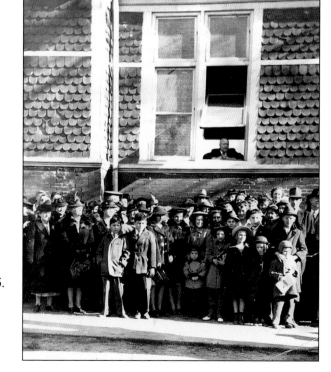

This photograph shows a Sunday school class along the Disston Street elevation of Tacony Baptist Church west of Hegerman Street. The church was constructed in two phases: the original chapel in 1884 and the rear addition in 1915. Constructed entirely of recycled grindstones from the Disston Saw Works, the addition gave the church its nickname, the Grindstone Church.

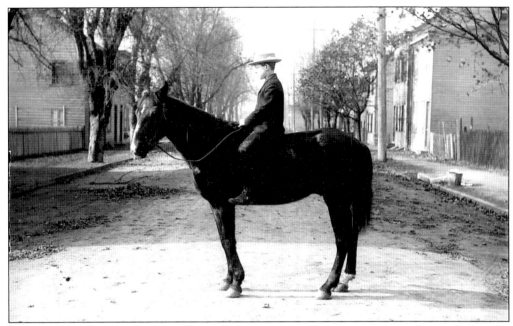

This *c.* 1900 photograph shows Frank Ramspacher perched atop a pony that is facing the Delaware River from in front of the family bakery at St. Vincent (now Wellington) and Wissinoming Streets. Pony rides and photographic opportunities were popular pastimes for many a child at the turn of the century.

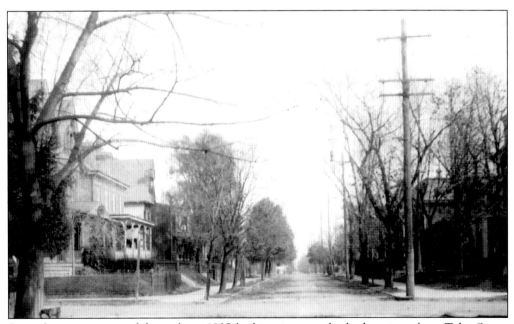

Seen above is a postcard from about 1905 looking in a northerly direction along Tulip Street from Disston Street. This section of Tacony is characterized by larger twin and detached single homes and in its earliest days was populated by executives and craftsmen employed at Disston Saw Works, which at its height employed over 3,500 people at its riverfront factory. (Courtesy of Dennis Lebofsky.)

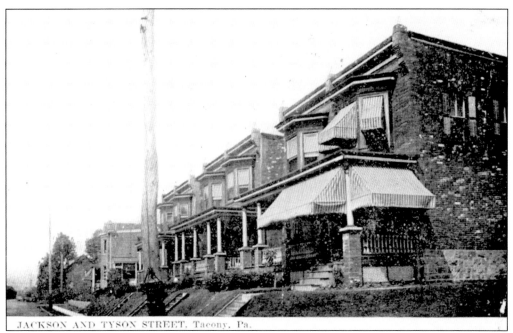

JACKSON AND TYSON STREET, Tacony, Pa.

The postcard seen above is likely from the 1920s and depicts three sets of semidetached residences situated along the westerly side of Jackson Street between Tyson Avenue and Disston Street. This block is perched along an area once known as the Mount for its high elevation and is situated in the northwesterly corner of the Henry Disston estate.

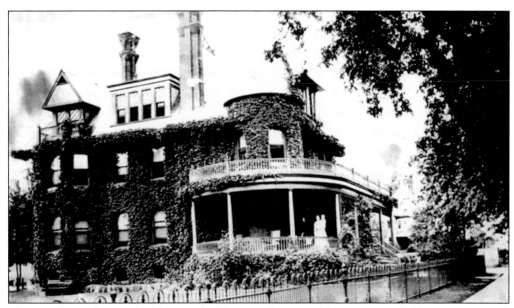

This pre-1920 photograph depicts the Disston Street residence of Frank Shuman, Tacony's notorious inventor, best known for patenting wire glass and experimenting with solar energy. *The Power of Light* (2003), by Frank T. Kryza III, extensively studies Shuman's solar energy exploits and credits Shuman with advancements in solar technology still in use today. (Courtesy of Connie Anderson.)

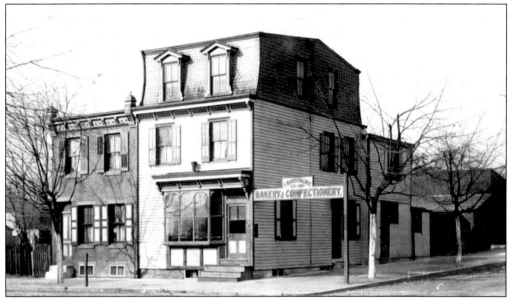

Ramspacher's Bakery was a thriving mom-and-pop bakery located at the southwest corner of Wissinoming and St. Vincent Streets (now Wellington Street) when this c. 1900 postcard was produced. Today, only two corners remain as the easterly side of Wissinoming Street is bounded by the southbound lanes of Interstate 95. Many commercial and residential uses in the shadow of the highway became fond memories by the late 1960s.

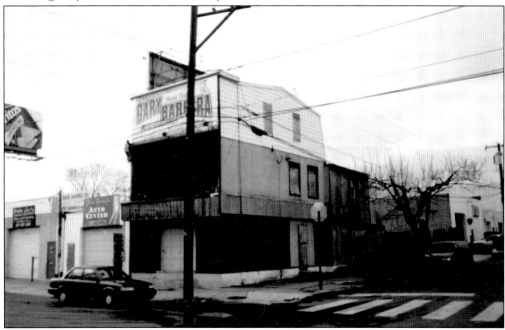

This is what the former Ramspacher's Bakery looks like today. No starker evidence exists than the before and after images of this building to depict the detrimental impact the construction of Interstate 95 has had on this part of Tacony. The Tacony Civic Association recently won a court decision affirming the city's zoning board decision to disallow the legalization of illegal billboards on this shell of a building. (Courtesy of Tacony Civic Association.)

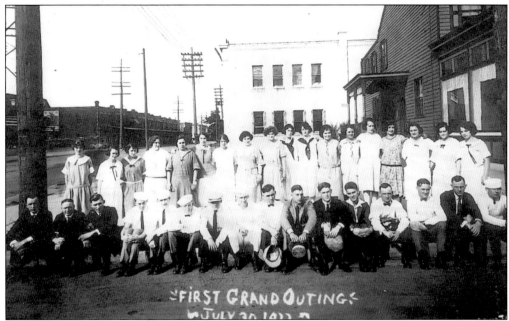

The 1921 image above is a group photograph from what was described as the First Grand Outing for this happy bunch of young men and women in Tacony. The photograph was taken from the southwest corner of Longshore and Torresdale Avenues, where today a branch of Sovereign Bank is located.

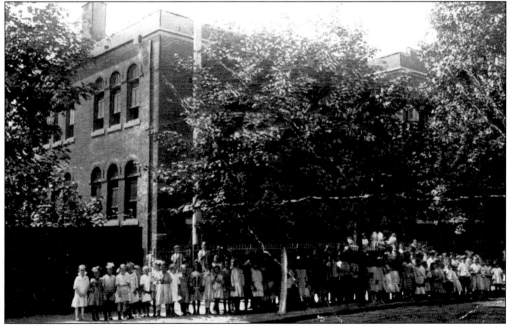

As the St. Leo the Great parish continued to grow in Tacony, an elementary school was established in 1908, enrolling 221 boys and girls in grades one through eight. This c. 1915 image shows children in front of the oldest portion of the school along Tulip Street. (Courtesy of Dennis Lebofsky.)

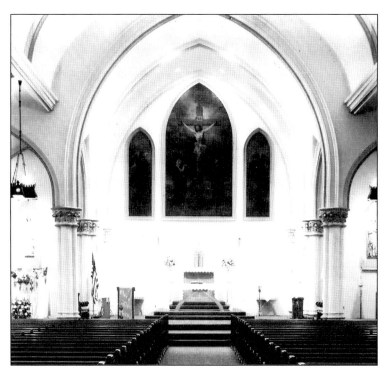

St. Leo the Great Roman Catholic Church first worshiped in St. Vincent's and then in temporary quarters at the New Era Printing House on State Road. The grand stone edifice at Unruh and Keystone Streets was built in stages beginning in 1884. The interior of this attractive church is seen here after renovations in the early 1980s.

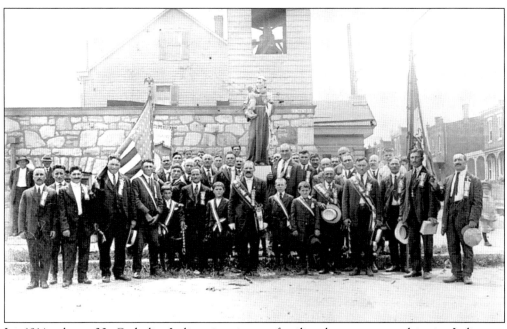

In 1914, about 30 Catholic Italian immigrant families began to worship in Italian at St. Vincent's. By 1917, Our Lady of Consolation was formed to fill the spiritual needs of this growing ethnic community. A stone edifice was constructed, which served as the parish home until 1928. Seen above is a group of parishioners celebrating the Feast of the Saints in front of the first church at Edmund and Wellington Streets.

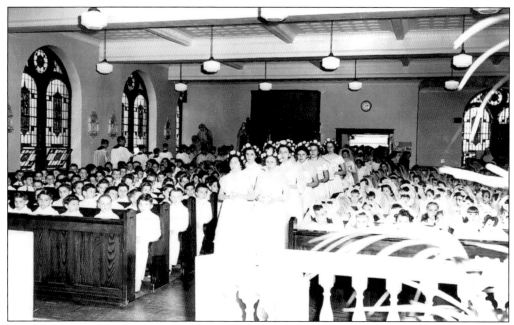

This photograph provides a rare glimpse at the interior of the second home of Our Lady of Consolation Church, which now serves as classrooms for the elementary school at the southeast corner of Princeton Avenue and Edmund Street. In 1956, the church moved to its present home on Tulip Street.

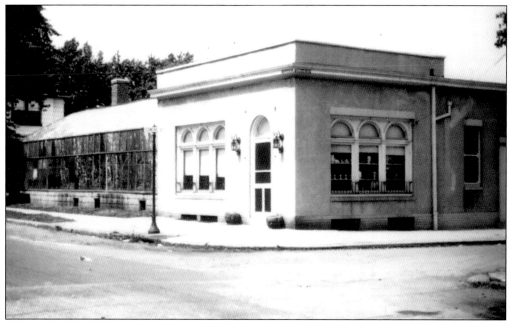

Ryan's Flower Shop, pictured in 1947, was a fixture for many years at the northwest corner of Tyson Avenue and Edmund Street. The building, with its rear greenhouse and pale green smooth stucco facade, was demolished in the 1980s. A series of duplexes is now on the site.

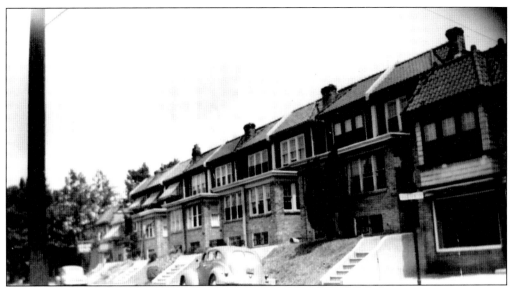

This 1947 photograph shows the northerly side of Longshore Avenue between Gillespie and Cottage Streets. As development in Tacony proceeded in a westerly direction after World War II, row-style residences became the style of choice among builders and homebuyers. These homes are characteristic of westerly portions of Tacony and most of Mayfair.

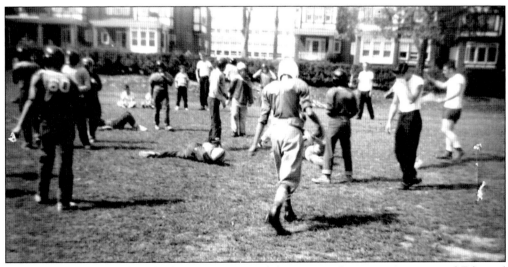

Russo Park is bounded by Bleigh Avenue, Torresdale Avenue, Cottman Avenue, and Edmund Street. Once known as Tacony Park, it was named in honor of Charles L. Russo, who built a machine company in the shadow of the park into three industries, including DeVal Corporation. Russo paid to illuminate the park at night for the youth of the area. Above are boys playing football in the park in 1957.

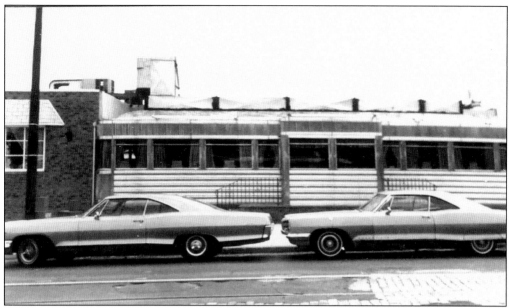

Leonard's Diner, seen above in the 1970s, was a popular dining spot for decades in Tacony. Situated south of Cottman Avenue along Torresdale Avenue, it was the kind of place where regulars could make a cup of coffee last all afternoon while the news and gossip of the day were discussed. The diner closed in the early 1980s, and a Dunkin' Donuts–Baskin Robbins facility is there today. (Courtesy of Rudy DeFinis.)

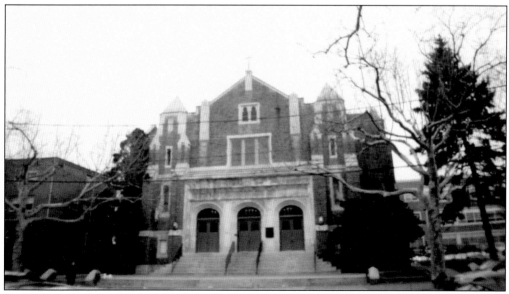

St. Hubert Catholic High School for Girls was established in 1941 in this building, which was originally used as an elementary school. This facility, located at the northwesterly corner of Torresdale and Cottman Avenues, has educated over 27,000 young women since opening. Today it is the largest Catholic girls' high school in Philadelphia, with students from 55 different elementary schools attending.

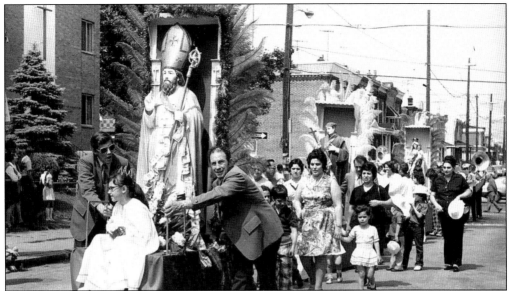

The photograph seen above was taken in 1974 along Tulip Street south of Princeton Avenue during the procession of the annual Feast of the Saints at Our Lady of Consolation. A still photograph of this group was memorialized in the mural commemorating the history of Italian Americans in Tacony, dedicated in 2002 along Torresdale Avenue near Cottman Avenue. The feast tradition continues at the parish to this day. (Courtesy of Our Lady of Consolation, photograph by Larry Trombetta.)

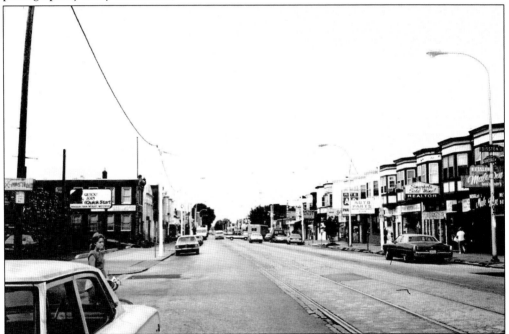

This view of Torresdale Avenue looks south from Disston Street in the mid-1980s. Septa's trolley line ceased to function in the early 1990s due to the deterioration of the metal support poles, wires, iron tracks, and Belgian blocks. Long a deterrent to pedestrian activity, the entire trolley infrastructure was removed in 2004 after vociferous community outcries.

Six

WISSINOMING

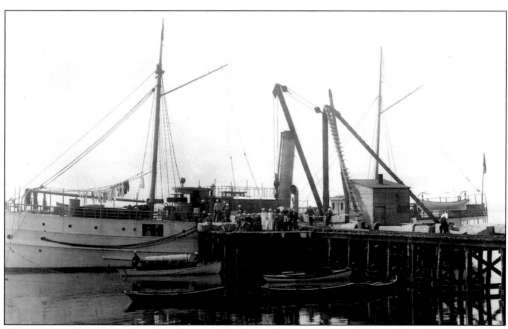

This postcard, captioned "The Floating Shad Hatchery," depicts a boat called *Fishhawk* docked at the Comly Street Wharf. In Wissinoming's old days, wild animals and rare birds could be found along the banks of the Delaware River and Wissinoming Creek, a tributary long since filled for development. As late as 1870, wolves were said to have crossed over the icy river to Wissinoming from New Jersey. (Courtesy of Tina Lamb.)

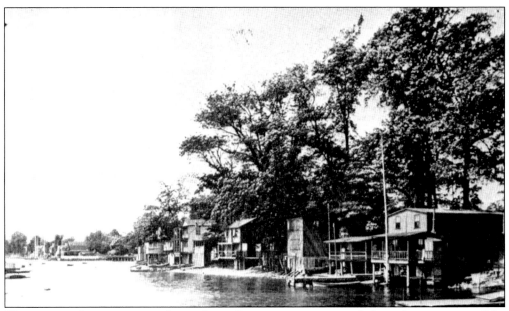

Wissinoming derives its name from a Lenni Lenape term meaning "where the grapes grow," for wild grapes once grew in densely wooded areas along the Wissinoming and Little Wissinoming Creeks. The tributaries that fed from the Delaware River no longer exist and were mostly in-filled to facilitate residential development. This view looks south along the Wissinoming riverfront. (Courtesy of Robert Morris Skaler.)

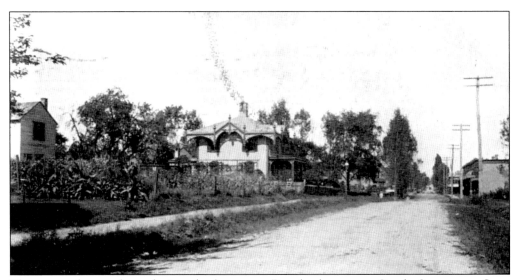

The postcard seen above depicts the long-gone Douglas house, on Comly Street near State Road, around 1910. This street was named for Harriet Comly, the wife of Robert Cornelius. One of Wissinoming's first residents, Cornelius bought 80 acres near Frankford and Cheltenham Avenues, extending back to what is now Comly Street. The famous photographer resided where Wissinoming Park is today. (Courtesy of Bruce Conner.)

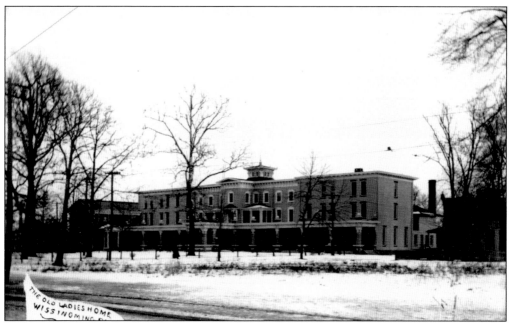

Shown above after a light snowfall around 1910, the Old Ladies' Home, established in 1875, was located south of Comly Street between the Delaware River and Tacony Street in Wissinoming. Locomotive manufacturing pioneer Matthias W. Baldwin had the building constructed in 1853 for use as his country estate.

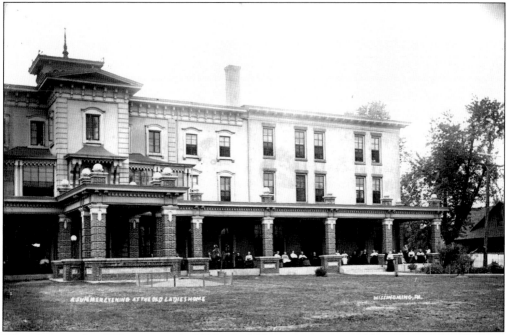

This photograph of Wissinoming's Old Ladies' Home was captioned by photographer William Sliker as "A Summer Evening at the Old Ladies' Home." Several dozen residents are pictured on the front porch. This facility remained until it was destroyed by fire in 1954. Industrial buildings and parking lots are present at the site today.

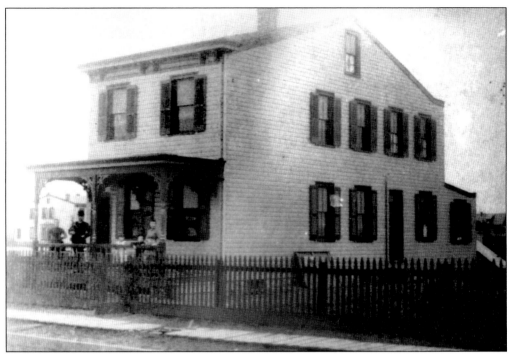

The above photograph dates from 1889 and depicts the house that still stands at 5717 Cottage Street, which is north of Cheltenham Avenue. Seen on the porch at the far right are Isabella and Edith Henderson. Edith was about six years old when the photograph was taken. Robert Henderson built the home so his family could move to Wissinoming from Kensington. Note the wooden sidewalk along Cottage Street. (Courtesy of Edith Bobb.)

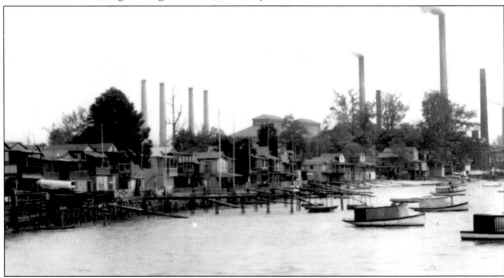

In Tacony and Wissinoming during the early 1900s, recreational uses coexisted with the industries that were blossoming between the Delaware River and Philadelphia-to-Trenton rail line. The Wissinoming waterfront is shown in a view looking north with long-forgotten boathouses lining the banks of the river and Lardner's Point Pumping Station in the distance. (Courtesy of Bruce Conner.)

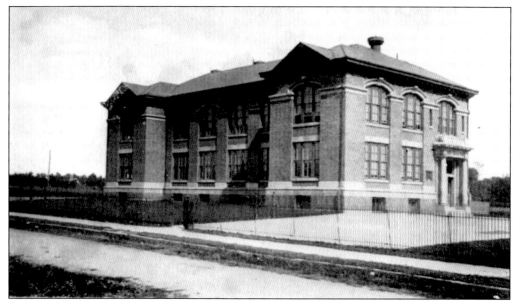

Wissinoming's first schoolhouse, at Jackson and Vankirk Streets, was built in 1888 and consisted of two rooms. Fourteen years later, the Henry W. Lawton School (shown here) was constructed to serve the community's growing population. The school was named for a Civil War colonel and Medal of Honor recipient who was killed during the Spanish-American War. Due to unsafe conditions, the school was rebuilt in 1974. (Courtesy of Tina Lamb.)

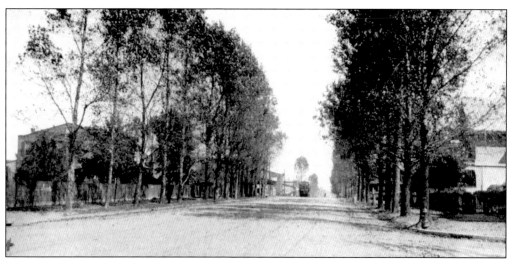

Seen above is a view of Torresdale Avenue in the old days. Some of the stores that lined the avenue in Wissinoming's bygone era include Gootman's Dry Goods, George Louie's Chinese Laundry, Kline's 5&10, J. Horace Eyre's Magazine & Tobacco Store, Howarth's Apparel, Dietrich's Florist, and Andy Newton's Chevrolet agency. (Courtesy of Robert Morris Skaler.)

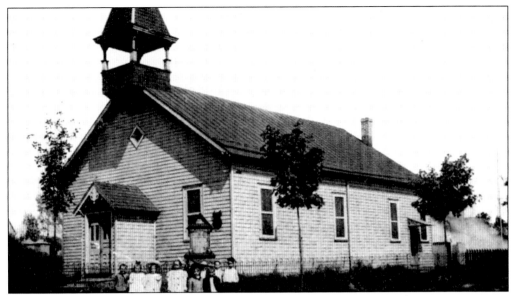

The Wissinoming United Methodist Church took shape around 1886, when prayer services were held in a house near Comly and Hegerman Streets. The congregation organized in 1888, and by 1893, the frame church seen above had been erected at Comly and Jackson Streets. In 1912, a granite church was completed with the frame section moved to the rear. A Sunday school building was erected in 1927. (Courtesy of Bruce Conner.)

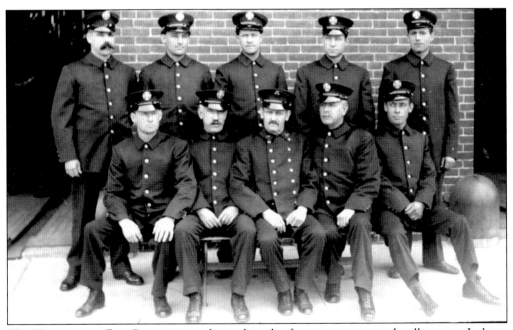

The Wissinoming Fire Company was housed in the former two-room schoolhouse at Jackson and Vankirk Streets. The above postcard depicts the town's firemen in 1909. The building had a stable at the rear for the horses that would pull the firefighting equipment in the old days. Now known as Engine 52 of the Philadelphia Fire Department, the modern-day firehouse was built in 1951 at the same location as the original. (Courtesy of Bruce Conner.)

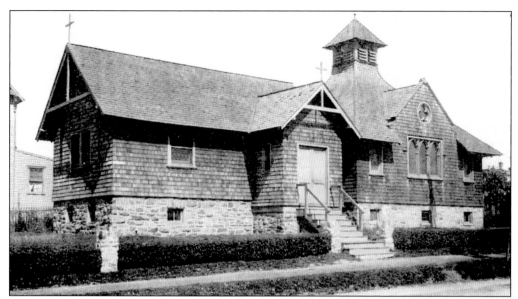

St. Bartholomew's Episcopal Church, at the corner of Ditman and Comly Streets, is seen above as it appeared before the stone addition was completed in 1928. The original edifice was erected in 1895, and the congregation's Women's Guild raised funds to help build the stone parish house. Wissinoming was dubbed Holy City in the old days due to the quantity of different houses of worship in a relatively small geographic area. (Courtesy of Tina Lamb.)

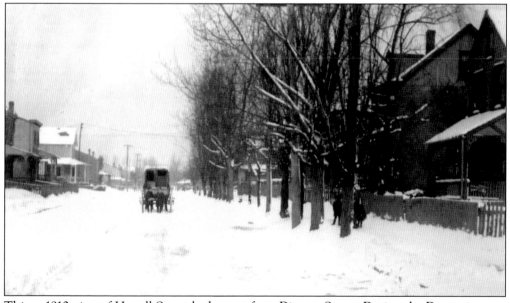

This c. 1910 view of Howell Street looks west from Ditman Street. During the Depression era, an inexpensive form of recreation was quoits, which involved the pitching of iron objects to steel pegs, anchored at opposite ends of a narrow court. Two popular clubs in Wissinoming were the Howell Quoit Club and the Benner Quoit Club. (Courtesy of Robert Morris Skaler.)

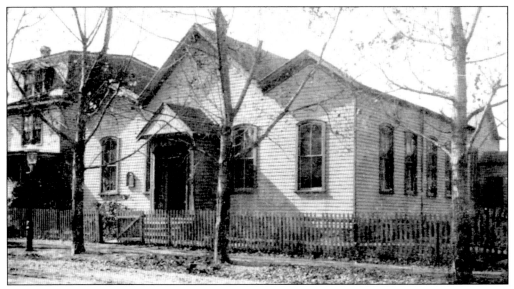

The Wissinoming Presbyterian Church began in a rented room used as a Sunday school. The congregation built a small frame chapel on Howell Street at Torresdale Avenue in 1886, and the church organized in 1888. A new church was built in 1920, and in 1946 the original church, used as a Sunday school building and depicted in the postcard above, was demolished. (Courtesy of Bruce Conner.)

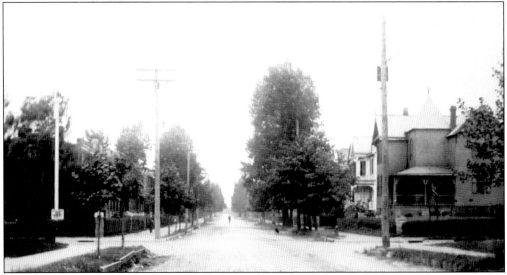

Comly Street at Ditman is pictured c. 1910. The course of development in Wissinoming took a similar path as Tacony, with residential housing springing up around 1880. Industry was concentrated along the riverfront, with a blend of row, twin, and single homes developed west of the railroad. Like Tacony, blocks in the westerly portion of Wissinoming are characterized by World War II–era row homes, which prevail in adjacent Mayfair. (Courtesy of Robert Morris Skaler.)

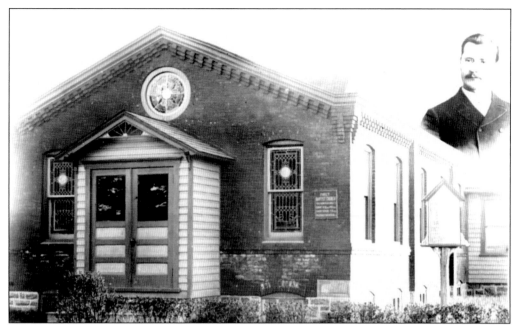

In 1899, the First Baptist Church of Wissinoming originated in the front room of a house on Howell Street. By 1901, the church shown here had been erected at the corner of Howell and Ditman Streets. In 1924, a new church building was constructed at Benner and Walker Streets. (Courtesy of Bruce Conner.)

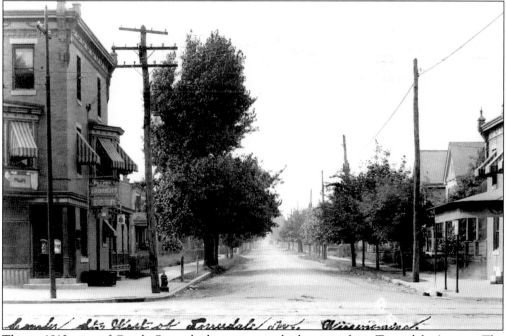

This c. 1910 view of Comly Street looks in a westerly direction from Torresdale Avenue. The bar on the left-hand side was at one time the only tavern in Wissinoming and has been in operation as a tavern since the early days. Today it is known as the Comly Café. (Courtesy of Bruce Conner.)

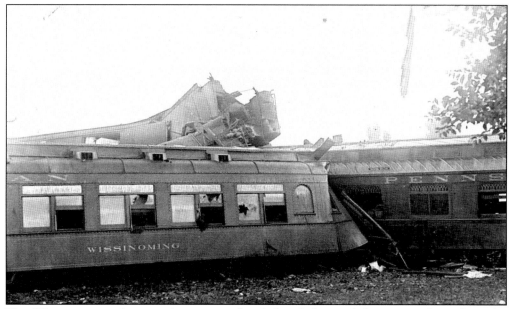

The Wissinoming rail car is shown in a derailed and dismantled state, resulting from the devastating windstorm of March 27, 1911. Many postcards depicted scenes from this event for years to come. Prior to this catastrophe, the last memorable weather event to impact the area was the year without a summer in 1816, when snow and ice fell and wiped out countless crops.

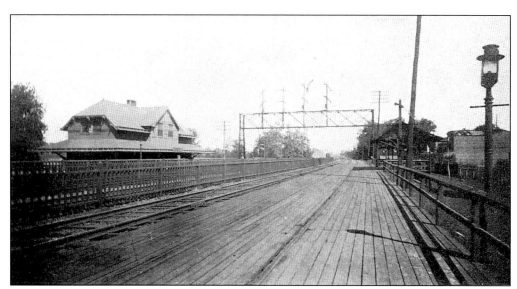

This c. 1900 view looks north along the tracks at the Wissinoming station. This neighborhood is no longer a passenger stop at this location, having been closed several years ago by Septa as part of budget cuts that cited lack of ridership. (Courtesy of Tina Lamb.)

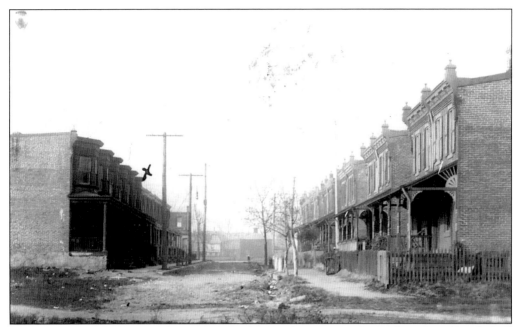

This c. 1900 view looks east along Homestead Street from Tacony Street (now State Road). Still intact today, Homestead Street is one of the few remaining residential streets east of Interstate 95. Industrial uses have dominated the area since the early part of the 20th century. (Courtesy of Tina Lamb.)

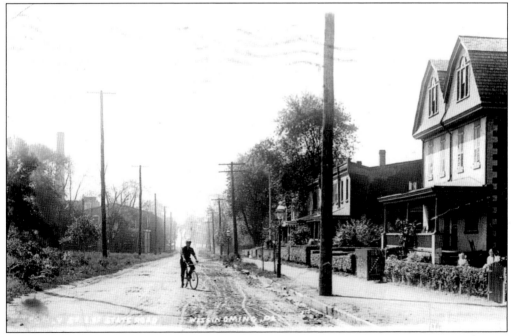

Looking east from State Road, this c. 1910 view of Comly Street includes an industrial smokestack in the distance. In Wissinoming's early years, extensive land along the riverfront was used as a staging area for drills by the mounted police. (Courtesy of Bruce Conner.)

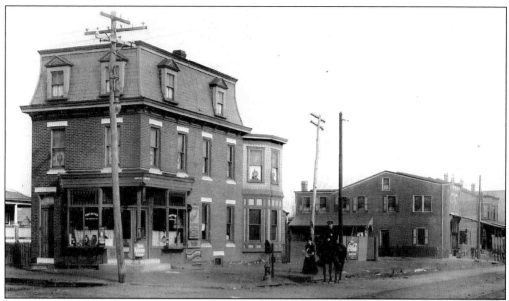

Seen above is a view of the corner of Howell Street and Torresdale Avenue, where Burtt's Drug Store doubled as Wissinoming's first post office. A new one-story post office was eventually constructed on Comly Street just east of Torresdale Avenue, and the facility stayed at this location until moving to a storefront at 5916 Torresdale Avenue in 1957. (Courtesy of Dennis Lebofsky.)

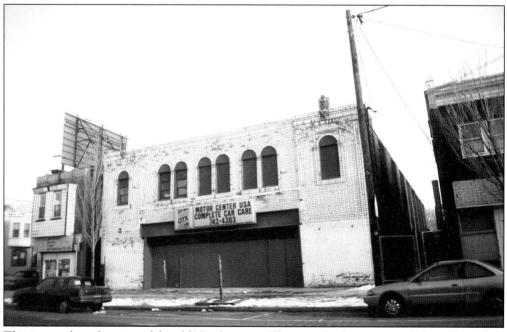

This is a modern-day view of the old Northeastern Theater, which was situated along Torresdale Avenue south of Benner Street. Fond memories of this theater, which was later called the Benner, include the 10¢ Saturday matinee to see anything ranging from cartoons to westerns to serials. Today the building is used for automobile repairs with the main entrance off Benner Street at the side.

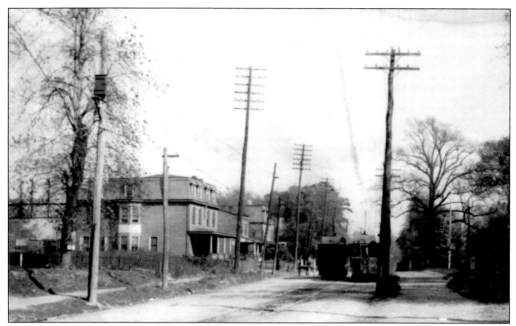

In addition to the installation of trolley lines and the construction of the Tacony-Palmyra Bridge, a major breakthrough that served to increase residential development in Wissinoming was the paving of Harbison Avenue from Cheltenham Avenue to Frankford Avenue in 1949. Seen above are two trolleys traveling along State Road around 1915. (Courtesy of Tina Lamb.)

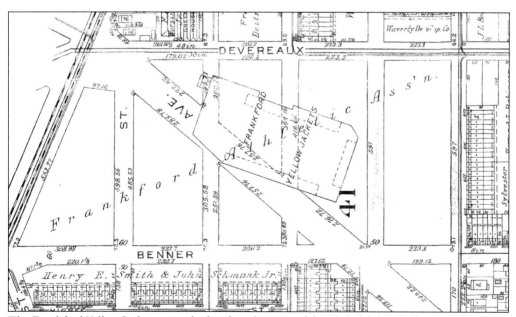

The Frankford Yellow Jackets were the local predecessor of the Philadelphia Eagles in the National Football League. Wissinoming was their home, and the team played games on a field located near Frankford Avenue and Devereaux Street. The team was founded by the Frankford Athletic Association in 1899, joined the National Football League in 1924, won the league championship in 1926, and disbanded in 1930.

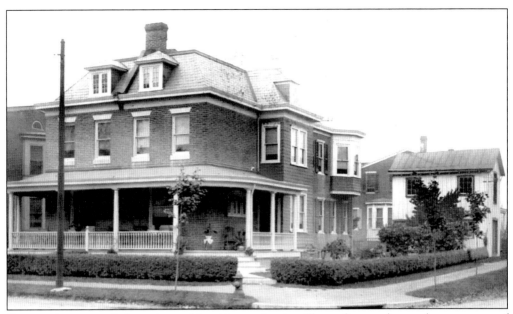

Seen in the postcard above is an old residence that is still standing at the southwest corner of Torresdale Avenue and Higbee Street. Like many of the older residences still lining the avenue that have been adapted over the years, this building today contains a one- and partial two-story extension at the front. This maximized the usage of the first floor for commercial use. (Courtesy of Tina Lamb.)

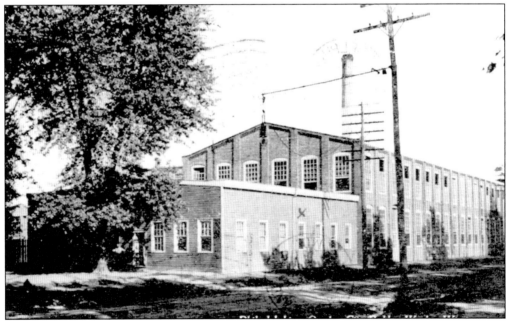

The Quaker City Rubber Company, seen above in a postcard from about 1910, was a major industry in Wissinoming in the early 1900s and was situated along the northerly side of Comly Street at the Delaware River. Like other industrial facilities in the area such as Philadelphia Cordage Works and National Ammonia Company, railroad tracks extended into the property for shipping products throughout the country. (Courtesy of Tina Lamb.)

Seven

THE BOULEVARD
AND BEYOND

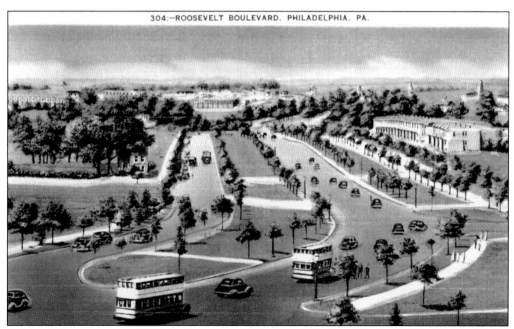

Roosevelt Boulevard (U.S. Route 1) was named for Pres. Theodore Roosevelt in 1920. Originally planned in a 1903 ordinance, this 12-mile, 300-foot-wide artery began at Broad Street and connected with the Pennypack Circle, leading to the main route of the Lincoln Highway to New York. Beyond the circle in this view is a double-decker bus traveling the boulevard.

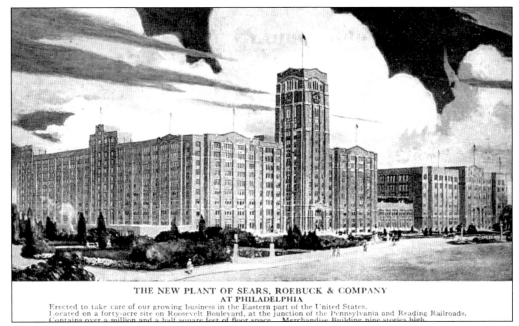

THE NEW PLANT OF SEARS, ROEBUCK & COMPANY
AT PHILADELPHIA
Erected to take care of our growing business in the Eastern part of the United States.
Located on a forty-acre site on Roosevelt Boulevard, at the junction of the Pennsylvania and Reading Railroads.
Contains over a million and a half square feet of floor space. Merchandise Building nine stories high.

The main plant of Sears, Roebuck & Company was an imposing presence on Roosevelt Boulevard's landscape and was situated at Adams Avenue, representing the unofficial gateway to the great Northeast from points south. The building was demolished with nostalgic fanfare in the 1990s to make way for a retail development featuring a Home Depot store. Today, the central tower is the only physical remnant of the site's storied past.

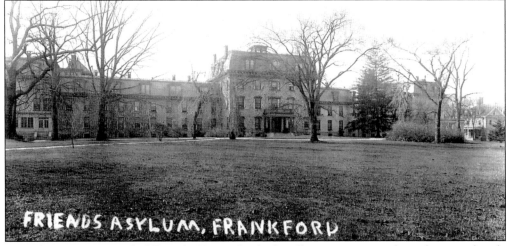

Seen above is a postcard of Friends' Hospital, which still occupies a site along the easterly side of Roosevelt Boulevard at Adams Avenue. It is renowned for its beautiful azalea gardens. The facility was originally established as Friends Asylum for the Insane, and the road leading to the facility from the east was known as Asylum Pike. (Courtesy of Dennis Lebofsky.)

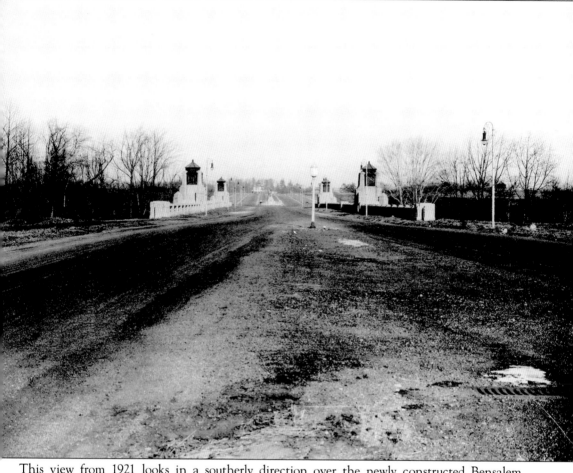

This view from 1921 looks in a southerly direction over the newly constructed Bensalem Avenue bridge over the Pennypack Creek. Four decorative towers, placed at each corner, were composed of poured concrete with stained-glass domelike roofs and iron gates leading to a small, enclosed room within. When Roosevelt Boulevard was widened to 12 lanes from 1963 to 1964, the towers were demolished and poured concrete encased the original bridge on both sides. When asked by a reporter why the towers were not salvaged in the reconstruction, the director of the Fairmount Park Commission replied, "They're just decorations. That's just the way they built bridges in those days. They never had any purpose."

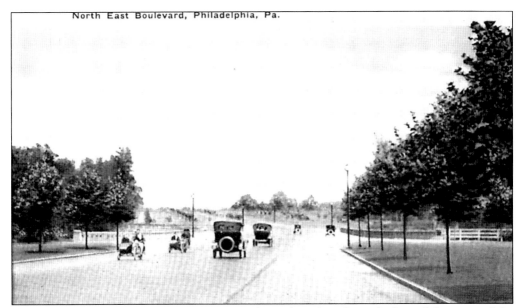

The postcard shown above, depicting Roosevelt Boulevard in the early days of the automobile, is captioned as Northeast Boulevard, which was only one of its popular names prior to being named for Theodore Roosevelt. In its earliest days, the roadway was also known as the Bensalem Boulevard or Torresdale Boulevard. (Courtesy of David A. Rizzo.)

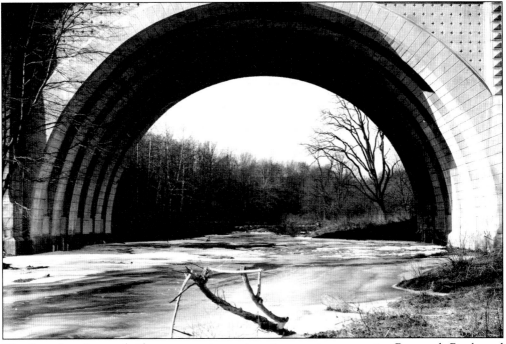

The Bensalem Avenue bridge was a major engineering step in connecting Roosevelt Boulevard with Lincoln Highway (U.S. Route 1) to New York. Originally 80 feet wide to accommodate six lanes of traffic, the center span (pictured in a view looking south) was 100 feet in diameter. The length of the bridge was 590 feet, and the spans at each side were 60 feet in diameter.

As evidenced by this postcard depicting 5919 Roosevelt Boulevard, houses along this roadway were made available for lodging in the pre-motel era. This advertisement for a stone-front row home was for Mrs. Edna Lange's Guest Home, which touted itself as Philadelphia's most modern guest home. (Courtesy of Tina Lamb.)

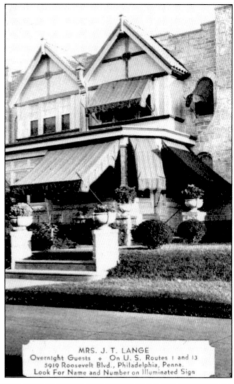

MRS. J. T. LANGE
Overnight Guests • On U. S. Routes 1 and 13
5919 Roosevelt Blvd., Philadelphia, Penna.
Look For Name and Number on Illuminated Sign

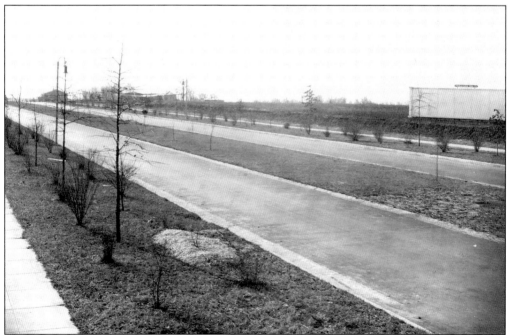

Seen above in its early days is the stretch of Roosevelt Boulevard from the Bensalem Avenue bridge, looking in a southerly direction toward the Pennypack Circle. Even in its infancy, this major roadway was not immune to billboards, as evidenced by the blank Philadelphia Sign Company installation on the right of the photograph.

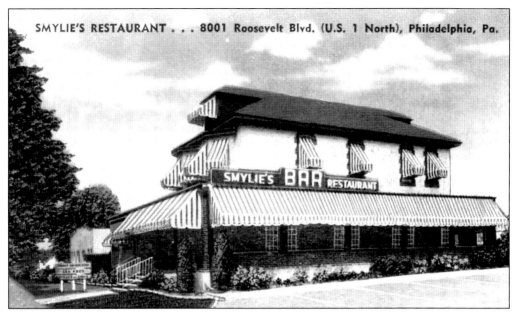

SMYLIE'S RESTAURANT . . . 8001 Roosevelt Blvd. (U.S. 1 North), Philadelphia, Pa.

This two-story restaurant-bar facility known as Smylie's was situated at the northeast corner of Roosevelt Boulevard and Rhawn Street. The Smylie family is renowned as the longtime publishers of the *Northeast Times* newspaper, which serves this section of the city. On this site today is the Smylie Times Office Building and a Checkers restaurant. (Courtesy of Tina Lamb.)

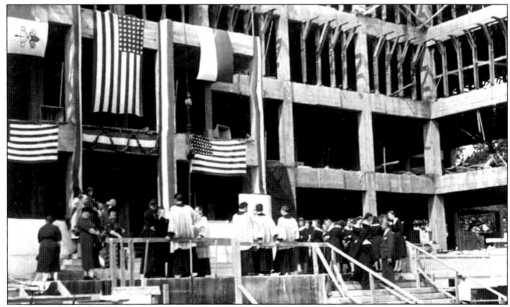

The Sisters of the Holy Family of Nazareth purchased a large site—extending from James McKinley's property east of Roosevelt Boulevard along Holme Avenue to the Pennypack Creek—and established Nazareth Hospital. Seen above during its 1939 dedication, the establishment of this hospital was a sure sign that Northeast Philadelphia had come into its own. Over the years, the facility has spawned nearby medical office development. (Courtesy of Dolores Franecke.)

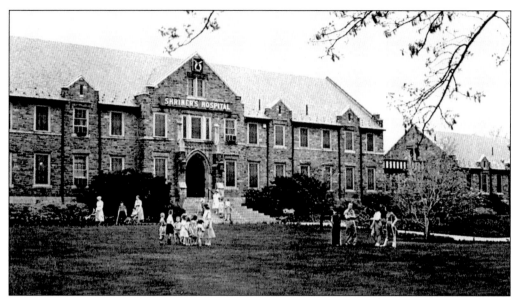

Shriners Hospital for Crippled Children was located along Roosevelt Boulevard's westerly side, north of Pennypack Circle. The hospital was owned and operated by the Order of the Mystic Shrine, who admitted any handicapped child regardless of race, color, or religion. This postcard stated that the facility was 100 percent charity and received nothing from the federal, state, or municipal governments. The building was demolished to facilitate medical office development. (Courtesy of Tina Lamb.)

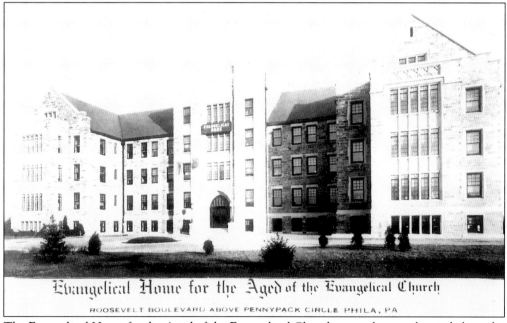

Evangelical Home for the Aged of the Evangelical Church

ROOSEVELT BOULEVARD ABOVE PENNYPACK CIRCLE PHILA, PA

The Evangelical Home for the Aged of the Evangelical Church, seen above, is located along the easterly side of Roosevelt Boulevard, north of the Pennypack Circle. Within two decades of the construction of the Bensalem Avenue bridge, institutional uses like these—including Shriners Hospital and Nazareth Hospital—sprung up to serve the expanding population of Northeast Philadelphia. (Courtesy of Dennis Lebofsky.)

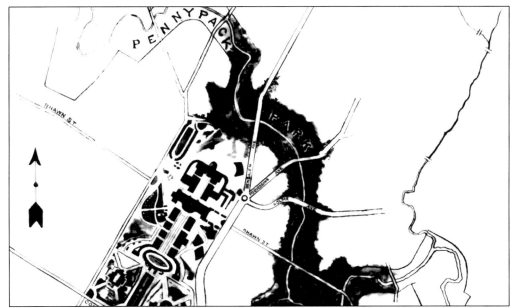

In 1921, the Tacony Manufacturers' Association, a group of motivated businessmen, made an ambitious and detailed proposal to stage the 1926 Sesquicentennial Exposition in Northeast Philadelphia. Envisioned on ground situated between Cottman Avenue, Pennypack Park, Roosevelt Boulevard, and Castor Avenue, this event (outlined in the map above) would have drastically changed the evolutionary course of Northeast Philadelphia.

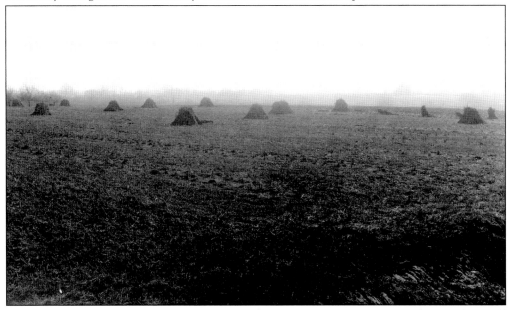

This view looks southeast from Solly and Bustleton Avenues in 1921, when farmland was all one could see. The photograph was taken from the northwesterly periphery of the proposed Sesquicentennial Exposition site. Infrastructure improvements envisioned in the proposal included three separate railroad spurs, extension of the Frankford elevated line along Bustleton Avenue from Bridge Street, and an elevated high-speed line through Pennypack Park from the mouth of the Delaware River north of Rhawn Street.

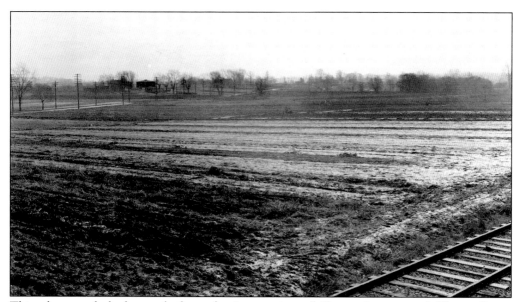

This photograph looks south from the intersection of Castor Avenue and Rhawn Street and was taken as part of the ultimately rejected proposal to hold the 1926 Sesquicentennial Exposition in Northeast Philadelphia. Held at League Island and undeveloped parts of South Philadelphia, this event was generally viewed as a disappointment, with the number of visitors falling way below expectations. Municipal (later John F. Kennedy) Stadium was constructed for this event.

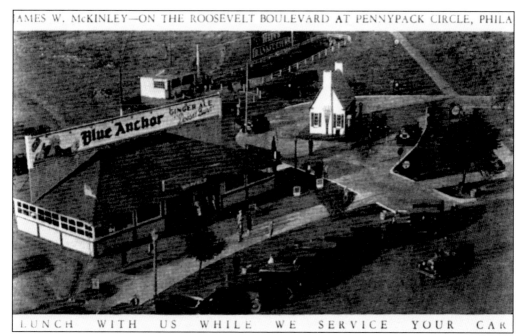

James W. McKinley's commercial operation was situated along the easterly side of Roosevelt Boulevard at the Poquessing Avenue extension at the Pennypack Circle. This postcard from the 1940s shows the Blue Anchor restaurant with a freestanding automobile service garage; it promoted the convenience offered if a patron needed car service. (Courtesy of David A. Rizzo.)

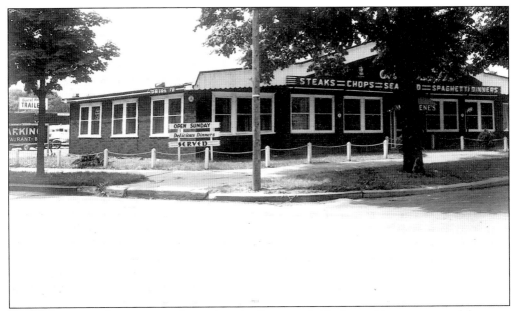

Gene's was a popular restaurant located at the Pennypack Circle, and it was operated for years by proprietor Gene Boeing. The restaurant's printed advertisements read, "The last stop for fine food before leaving Philadelphia . . . specializing in seafood, steaks, chicken and spaghetti dinners." The facility is shown here in the 1940s. (Courtesy of Dennis Lebofsky.)

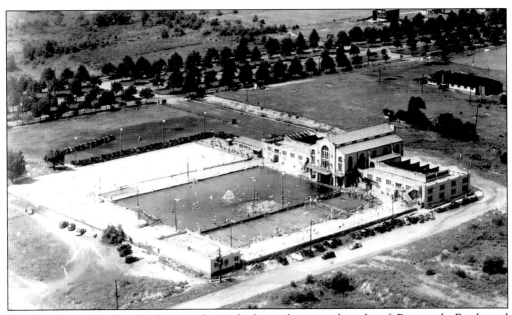

The Boulevard Pools, which were located along the easterly side of Roosevelt Boulevard between Tyson Avenue and St. Vincent Street, were in operation from the 1930s through the 1970s. Popular events held at this facility included Saturday night dances. The site is now occupied by a K-Mart retail store and W.O.W. Family Fun Center (originally United Skates of America). (Courtesy of Donna Dizierza, photograph by Frank Wilding.)

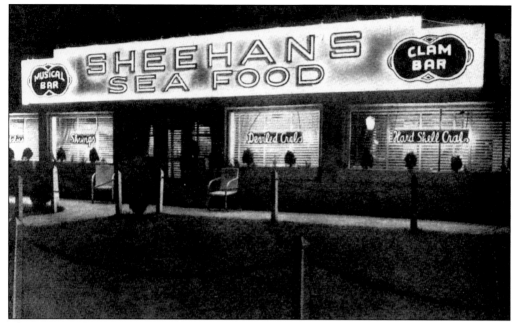

This postcard, believed to be from the 1940s, advertises Sheehan's, located along the westerly side of Roosevelt Boulevard at Hartel Street. The advertisement calls Route 1 the Maine-to-Florida Highway and states that all water used for drinking and cooking was from the restaurant's own artesian wells. (Courtesy of Tina Lamb.)

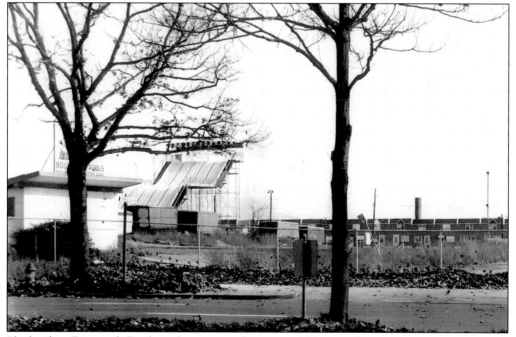

Playland on Roosevelt Boulevard was a popular carnival-like spot for summertime recreation. It was situated along the easterly side of Roosevelt Boulevard, north of Tyson Avenue, in the 1960s and 1970s. The perfect warm-weather complement to the adjacent Boulevard Pools, the facility is pictured not long before it closed in the 1970s. (Courtesy of Rudy DeFinis.)

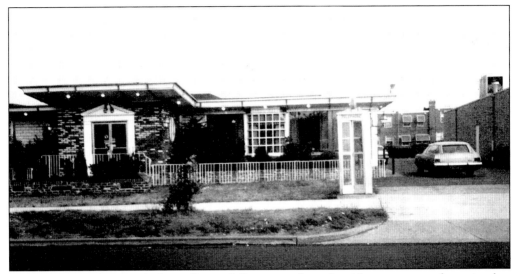

This mid-1970s photograph shows Greiner's Diner, another of a wide assortment of eateries that lined Roosevelt Boulevard. The diner was situated along the westerly side of the boulevard, just south of Cottman Avenue. A small office building is situated on the site today.

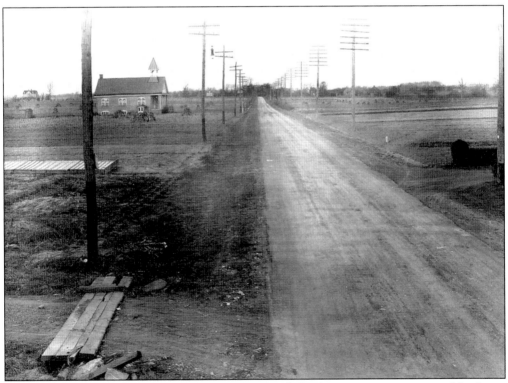

A solitary church is shown at what is now one of the busiest intersections in Northeast Philadelphia. The view looks north along Bustleton Avenue from Cottman Avenue, where today one would find the sprawling Roosevelt Mall to the right. A Sears and cinema complex are now to the left.

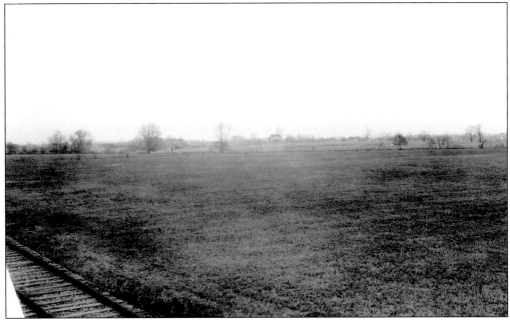

At the southwest corner of what is today Philadelphia's third largest shopping district, the intersection of Castor and Cottman Avenues looks much different today than it does in this 1921 photograph. Within a quarter-century, this area would experience unprecedented population growth. The trolley line in the foreground was long ago replaced by a bus route.

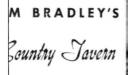
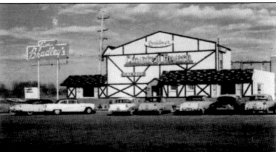
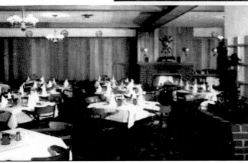
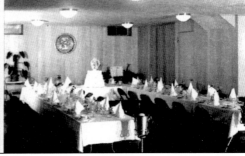

Jim Bradley's Country Tavern was located near the southeast corner of Bustleton and Cottman Avenues and at one time possessed a commanding view of the open fields that stood where Roosevelt Mall was eventually constructed across Cottman Avenue. This restaurant had several subsequent incarnations and was demolished to make way for a Circuit City store. (Courtesy of Tina Lamb.)

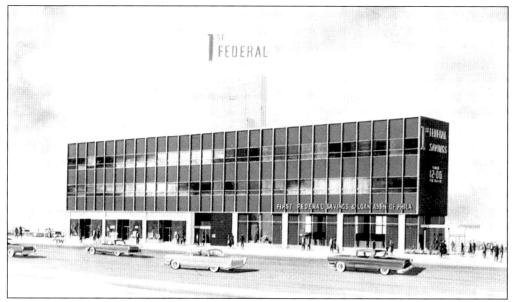

Seen above is the building situated at the northwest corner of Castor and Cottman Avenues. The building was originally constructed for use as the First Federal Savings Building, and for years it featured the familiar digital clock with the phrase "Time to Save." The back of this postcard, issued in the 1950s, touts the offices of Pennsylvania's oldest Federal Savings in the only ultramodern office building in Greater Northeast Philadelphia. (Courtesy of Tina Lamb.)

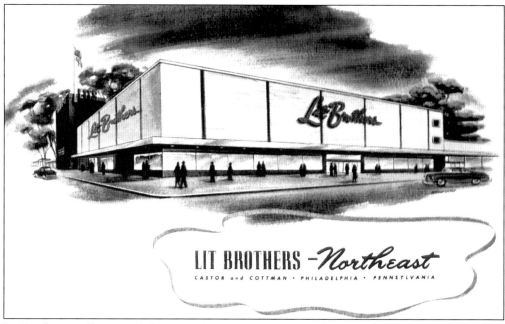

Lit Brothers, at Castor and Cottman Avenues, was promoted as one of America's most modern department stores in the heart of the Delaware Valley. The development of this store, along with Gimbel's (at Cottman and Bustleton Avenues) and the Roosevelt Mall (at Roosevelt Boulevard), solidified this area as a retail mecca to serve the dense and loyal residential communities sprouting up on all sides. (Courtesy of Dennis Lebofsky.)

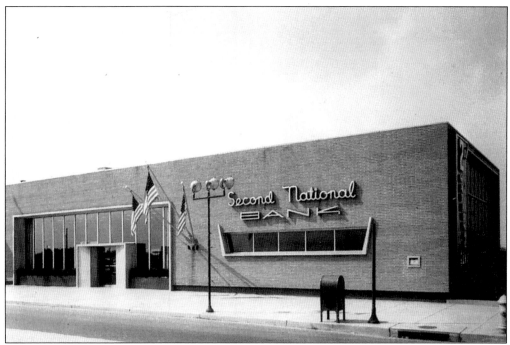

Cottman Avenue, from Roosevelt Boulevard to Castor Avenue, transformed from farmland to a major shopping area in about a 25-year span. Despite turnover—John Wanamaker's at Roosevelt Mall is now Strawbridge's, Gimbel's is now Sears, and Second National Bank (seen at Cottman Avenue and Horrocks Street) is now PNC Bank—this area remains strong, with high levels of occupancy. (Courtesy of Dennis Lebofsky.)

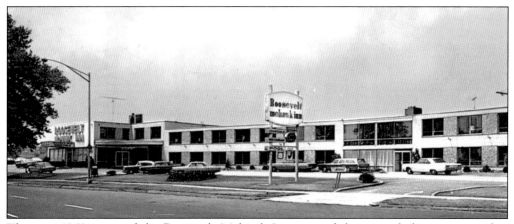

This is a 1960s view of the Roosevelt Mohawk Inn, one of the many lodging options that became popular in the mid-20th century. Now known as Roosevelt Motor Inn, the property is located along the westerly side of Roosevelt Boulevard north of Cottman Avenue. A similar facility known as Mohawk Motor Inn was located farther south along Roosevelt Boulevard.

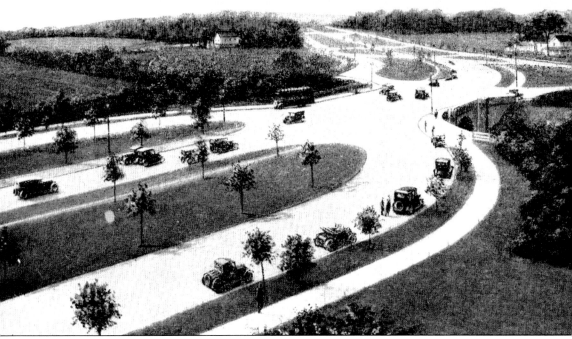

Roosevelt Boulevard is shown in a view looking south toward Pennypack Circle from about the Bensalem Avenue bridge. Since its widening to 12 lanes, this roadway has become infamous as a dangerous thoroughfare, especially at grade-level intersections. In 2001, 23 people died in accidents along Roosevelt Boulevard, with about six accidents per day reported. This led to a proposal to install red-light cameras at three locations (Cottman Avenue, Grant Avenue, and Red Lion Road along Roosevelt Boulevard). The first was installed in early 2005, and on the first day it photographed 254 cars proceeding illegally through red traffic lights. City and state officials hope the cameras will serve to reduce the number of fatalities and accidents along this major roadway.

Eight

MAYFAIR

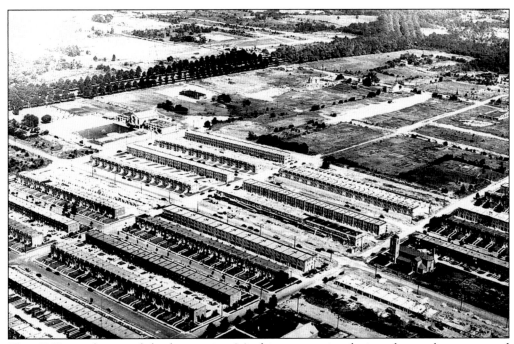

This 1947 aerial view of the burgeoning Mayfair community depicts the newly constructed homes between Longshore Avenue (on the left) and Cottman Avenue (on the right). Note St. John's Evangelical Lutheran Church (in the lower right-hand corner) and the Boulevard Pools (on the upper left-hand side). The treelined Roosevelt Boulevard extends into the upper right-hand corner. (Courtesy of St. John's Evangelical Lutheran Church.)

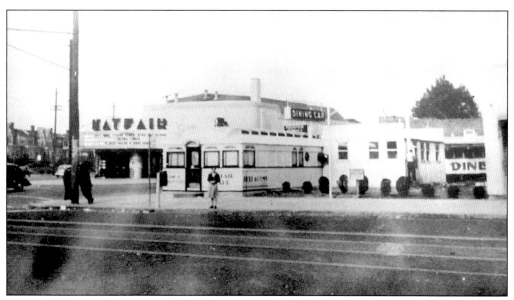

Mayfair's name is believed to have originated as a means for civic and business interests to differentiate the community blossoming west of Frankford Avenue from the established areas of Holmesburg and Tacony. At a 1928 community meeting, civic leader Thomas Donahue said, "We may fare well if we get behind this community . . . so why not call it Mayfair?" This photograph shows the Mayfair cinema and the Mayfair Diner's original location at Ryan Avenue. (Courtesy of Rudy DeFinis.)

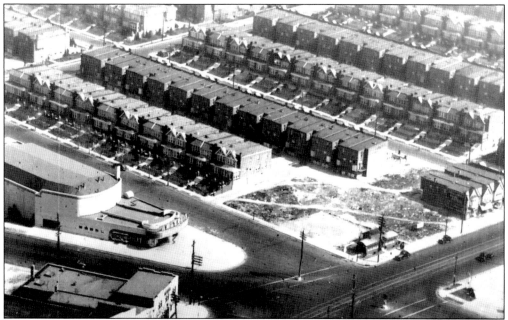

The development of the Market-Frankford Elevated Railway and Tacony-Palmyra Bridge in the 1920s had a direct impact on the establishment of Mayfair in the following decade. As westerly portions of Tacony became built up, developers looked to Mayfair as the next area where open fields could yield blocks and blocks of tidy row houses. Seen above is an aerial view of the Frankford-Cottman area in the 1950s. (Courtesy of Rudy DeFinis.)

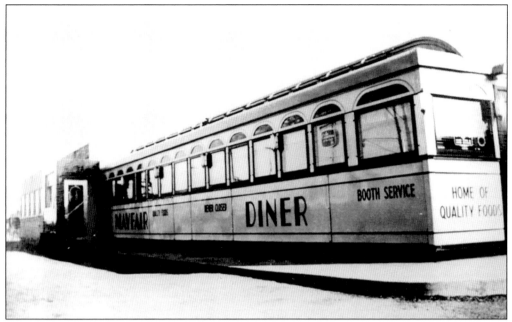

The Mayfair Diner is shown not long after it moved to its present location, bounded by Frankford Avenue, Bleigh Avenue, and Tudor Street. The diner moved one block south and was situated on the periphery of a rapidly developing residential area on the grounds of the old Forrest Home. (Courtesy of Rudy DeFinis.)

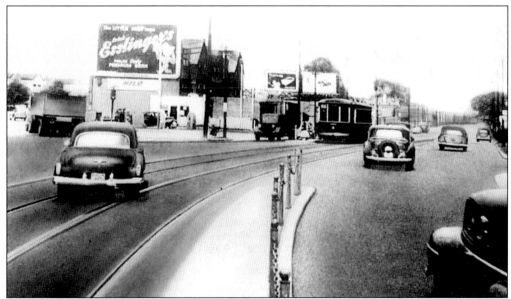

Although the buildings lining Frankford Avenue had been constructed for several years, it was not until the mid-1930s, after outcries from Mayfair businessmen, that the bed of trolley tracks in the center of the avenue were in-filled to allow unrestricted pedestrian access to all businesses. Until that time, only trolley-stop intersections contained paved crosswalks. Seen above is Frankford Avenue looking north at its junction with Rowland Avenue. (Courtesy of Rudy DeFinis.)

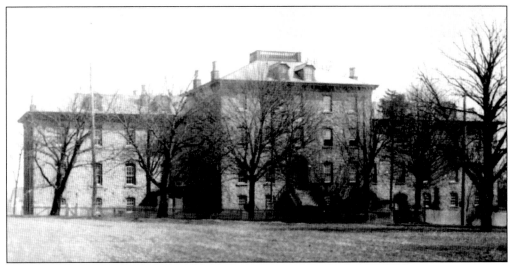

The Oxford and Lower Dublin Poor House was built around 1820 at the rear portion of grounds now occupied by Abraham Lincoln High School on Rowland Avenue. Managed by the City of Philadelphia, its operation was funded by a poor tax. The original building caught fire in 1854 and was replaced by the one seen here. Another fire led to its ultimate demolition in 1954. (Courtesy of Tina Lamb.)

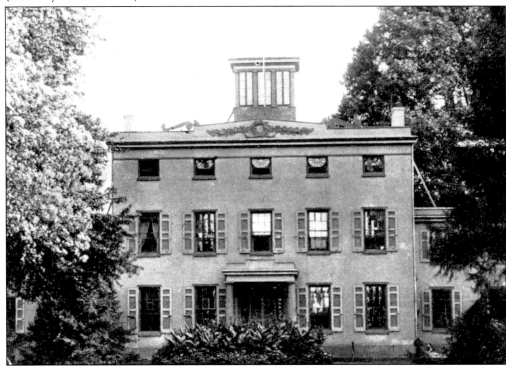

The Edwin Forrest Home for Aged Actors and Actresses was originally known as Spring Brook and was about 50 years old when purchased by the famous Philadelphia actor. Forrest aspired to help in perpetuity his fellow actors and actresses by stating in his will that 12 retired performers at a time will rest comfortably as long as they lived. Upon Forrest's death in 1872, actor William B. Lourdes became its first occupant.

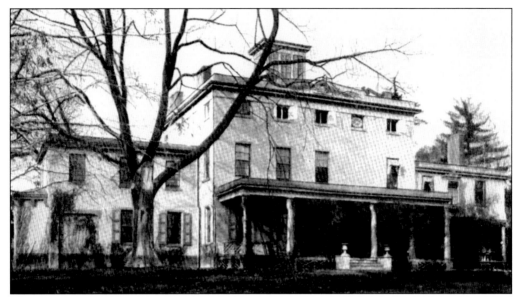

The Forrest Home boasted views of the Delaware River from its location perched near Frankford Avenue between Cottman Avenue and Sheffield Street. The property also had rare varieties of trees, flowers, and fruit groves on its grounds. One of its most famous visitors was Harry Houdini, who arrived in a black cape and wide-brimmed hat. By the 1920s, the property was sold to a developer for home construction and was demolished. (Courtesy of Dennis Lebofsky.)

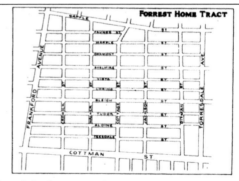

The advertisement seen here was produced for a local magazine and shows the division of the Forrest Home Tract into what would amount to 53 blocks yielding thousands of row homes and the Edwin Forrest Elementary School. An article in 1925 stated that the project would doubtless mean the establishment of this section of Frankford as a distinct modern community. The name Mayfair would come into vogue several years later.

One of the best tracts of ground available for dwelling house operations, on the site of the Edwin Forrest Home, is about to be offered to builders in entire blocks.

This development takes in Cottman, Bleigh, Shelmire, Napfle and other intermediate streets from Frankford Avenue to Dittman Street, including Erdrick, Walker, Cottage and Jackson Streets.

Besides being within convenient distance of the Roosevelt Boulevard on the west, and just around the corner from Torresdale Avenue on the east, this development taps a large industrial section employing many thousands of people and is one of the best opportunities for dwelling operations in the northeast, water, sewer and gas being already in in the immediate vicinity.

121

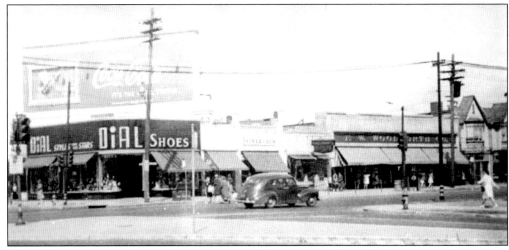

This 1950s photograph shows the intersection of Cottman and Frankford Avenues, the gateway to Mayfair and perhaps the most recognizable intersection in Northeast Philadelphia. Pat's Music Store is today located where Dial Shoes is seen above. Also at this intersection was the Mayfair cinema, which closed in the 1980s and is now occupied by an Eckerd retail store and pharmacy.

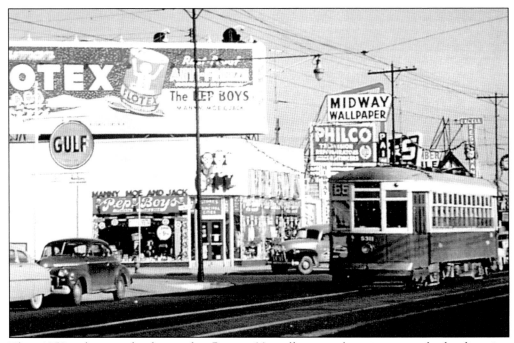

This 1950s photograph shows the Route 66 trolley traveling in a southerly direction along Frankford Avenue. The location is at the westerly corner of Friendship Street, where a Pep Boys once stood. In recent years, the property has been occupied as a Dollar Store. (Courtesy of Rudy DeFinis.)

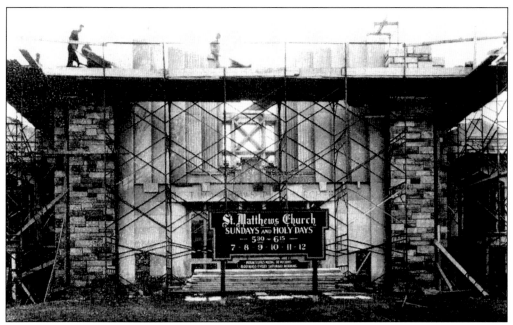

St. Matthew's Roman Catholic Church was established in the 1940s to fill a need for the many Catholics moving into the rapidly growing Mayfair community. The church is located at the southeast corner of Cottman Avenue and Battersby Street. Seen above are workers finishing the upper level of this stone-constructed facility. (Courtesy of Rudy DeFinis.)

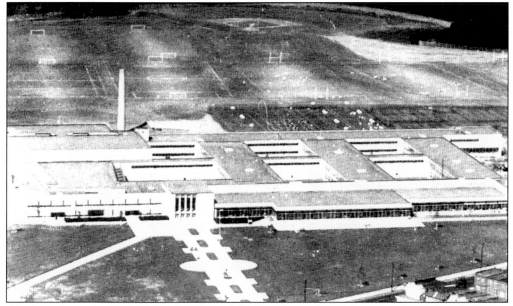

Abraham Lincoln High School and its fields are located on the grounds of the old Lower Dublin and Oxford Poor House. Seen above after its construction, from 1948 to 1949, the school filled the void of a public high school for the area's expanding population. Although it was originally going to be called Mayfair High School, opposition from groups of Holmesburg and Tacony residents led the school board to choose the name Lincoln instead. (Courtesy of Dennis Lebofsky.)

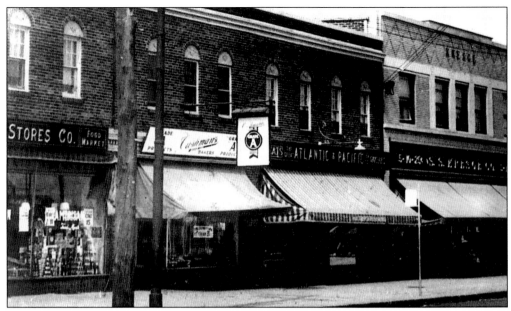

Seen above is a 1930s view of the westerly side of Frankford Avenue, just south of its intersection with Cottman Avenue. Cottman Avenue got its name from the family that held farmland in the early days of Northeast Philadelphia near Bustleton Avenue and Township Line Road. The former name of Cottman Avenue was Township Line Road, which represented the dividing line between Oxford and Lower Dublin Townships. (Courtesy of Rudy DeFinis.)

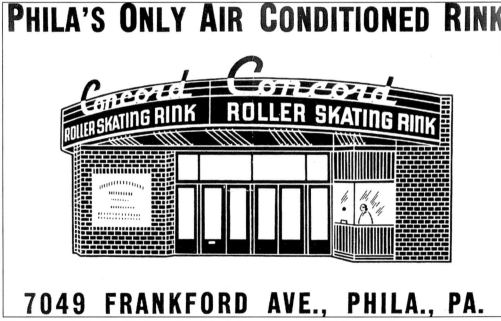

The Concord Skating Rink, on Frankford Avenue south of Princeton Avenue, was a highly popular gathering spot for local youths. There were more than a few married couples who could tell how they met their spouse at the Concord. The rink closed in the 1980s, and the site is now occupied by a self-storage facility. (Courtesy of Rudy DeFinis.)

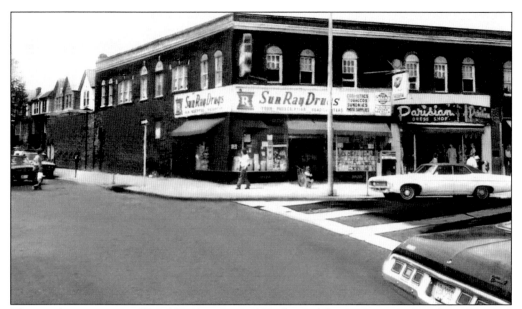

The northwest corner of Franklin Avenue and Englewood Street is pictured in the 1970s. Sun Ray Drugs was a traditional pharmacy chain where one could pay utility bills, get a money order, or stop at the ice-cream fountain. This convenient spot was situated midway between the Mayfair and Merben movie theaters, which for many years filled the entertainment needs of residents prior to the advent of multiplex cinemas.

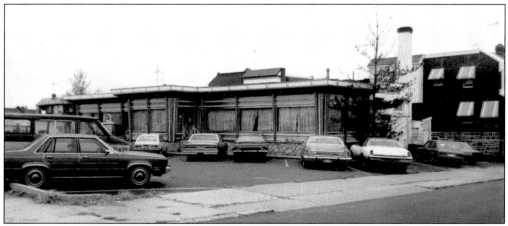

From the days of Mayfair's early development through the early 1980s, the Satellite Diner, as it was once known, provided another dining option for hungry patrons after a night at the movies or Concord Skating Rink. Seen above is the diner in its last days at the southeast corner of Frankford Avenue and Vista Street. An office building is on the site today. (Courtesy of Rudy DeFinis.)

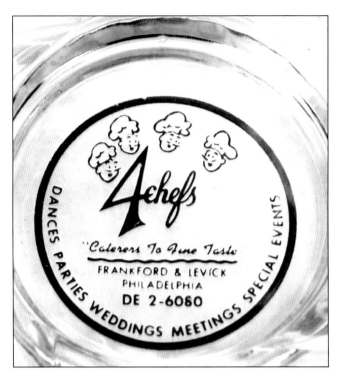

This ashtray advertises the old 4 Chefs catering facility, site of many catered events and fund-raisers over its many years of existence. This property was located along the westerly side of Frankford Avenue between Levick and Hellerman Streets. The building was demolished in the mid-1980s for the construction of Mayfair Center, a neighborhood shopping center anchored by a Shop & Bag supermarket. (Courtesy of Rudy DeFinis.)

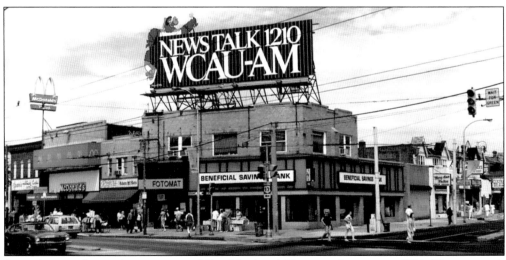

Seen above is the southwest corner of Frankford and Cottman Avenues in 1984. The avenue is bustling with activity during one of the summer sidewalk sales. This intersection has proven to be a popular gathering place for festive celebration at the moment of championship-clinching victories by Philadelphia sports teams. This tradition started after World War II when Northeast residents assembled here upon the victory of the Allies.

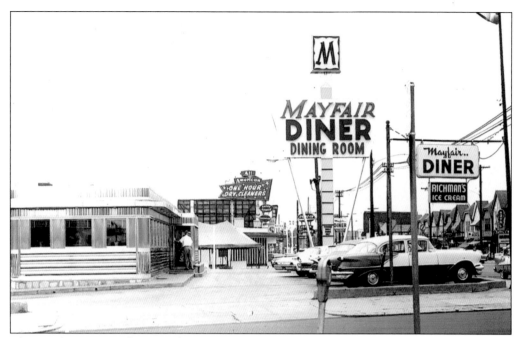

The Mayfair Diner is shown with its more familiar stainless-steel facade in the late 1950s. Signs reminiscent of the doo-wop era dominate this view of Frankford Avenue. One of the most memorable events at the Mayfair Diner in recent history was a stop by Bill Clinton before his election as president of the United States in 1992. Throngs of onlookers assembled for this well-publicized visit. (Courtesy of Rudy DeFinis.)

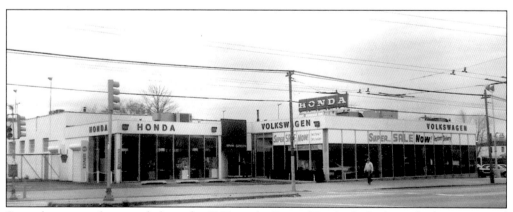

Seen above in a photograph from the 1980s is the Porter Honda dealership, which was situated along the easterly side of Frankford Avenue on about an acre of land and bounded by Unruh Avenue and Wells Street. Today the site is occupied by a branch of Commerce Bank, which purchased the property in 2002.

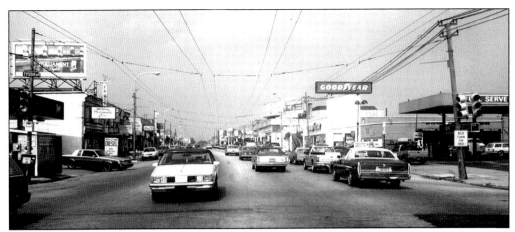

This 1991 photograph shows the northeast corner of Frankford and Tyson Avenues. The Exxon, Goodyear Tire, and McBride's facilities, with lower-level Playworld arcade and bingo hall, were demolished to facilitate the development of a Walgreen's. The growing popularity of convenience stores and mega-pharmacies has created up to three or four waves of development in an 80-year span at some sites along Frankford Avenue in Holmesburg and Mayfair.

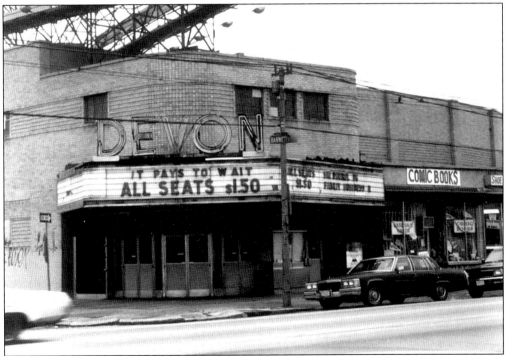

The Devon Theater, seen above in its waning days, was built in 1945. Located at Frankford Avenue and Barnett Street and being a first-run cinema for decades, the theater became an X-rated cinema in the 1970s, followed by a $1-per-ticket second-run theater. A modest revival in the late 1990s was short lived. The building has been purchased by the Mayfair Community Development Corporation for conversion into a performing arts theater. (Courtesy of Rudy DeFinis.)